IMAGES
of America

KENTUCKY'S
LOST BOURBON
DISTILLERIES

McKenna Distillery Postcard View. This early postcard shows off the picturesque buildings and grounds of the small McKenna Distillery, located near Fairfield in Nelson County. As with marketing for many distilleries then and today, the description emphasizes that the distillery's products are both "old fashioned" and "hand made." The distillery was founded in 1858 by Henry McKenna, an immigrant from County Derry in Ireland, and ceased operations around 1975, adding it to the long list of "lost" bourbon distilleries in Kentucky. (Joseph Seagram and Sons Photographs, UKSC.)

On The Cover: **Distillery Crew, 1890.** The workers at the R. Cummins & Co. Distillery turned out for this photograph taken in 1890. This crew was similar to others pictured throughout this book: from the booted men with slouch hats who did the manual labor to the men in coats and vests who worked in the office to keep up with the mountains of paperwork required in the distillery business. (Courtesy of the Oscar Getz Museum of Whiskey History.)

IMAGES
of America

KENTUCKY'S
LOST BOURBON
DISTILLERIES

Berkeley and Jeanine Scott

ARCADIA
PUBLISHING

Published by Arcadia Publishing
Charleston, South Carolina

Printed in the United States of America

Library of Congress Control Number: 2023933726

For all general information, please contact Arcadia Publishing:
Telephone 843-853-2070
Fax 843-853-0044
E-mail sales@arcadiapublishing.com
For customer service and orders:
Toll-Free 1-888-313-2665

Visit us on the Internet at www.arcadiapublishing.com

This book, like all our others, is dedicated to our immediate family:
sons Sean and Rob, daughter-in-law Rebecca, grandson Noah,
and granddaughter Alison. Also, we want to mention two other
family members we are close to: our niece Kristen and our nephew
Rex. And finally, even though they never will be able to read
this, we want to include our cats: Opus, Sylvie, and Stinky.

CONTENTS

ACKNOWLEDGMENTS

As we have said in past books, assembling almost 200 historical photographs is a task that requires the cooperation of lots of individuals and organizations. For this book, the people at the Special Collections Research Center at the University of Kentucky Libraries provided invaluable assistance, especially Sarah Coblentz, research services manager. We abbreviated the University of Kentucky Special Collections as UKSC and included the collection information for those photographs in most cases.

Nelson County historian Dixie Hibbs and the folks at the Oscar Getz Museum of Whiskey History in Bardstown were also very helpful, as usual. Also, as always, the photographs Olivia Ripy shared with us from the Ripy Family collection were invaluable in telling this story. Denny Lipscomb helped us by providing some great images of Harrison County distilleries. Cheers to Mandy Ryan at the Kentucky Distillers' Association and Tim Holz at the Brown-Forman Archives, who worked with us on using photographs from previous books on the Kentucky Bourbon Trail®. In addition, we received some excellent photographs from the Boone County Library and the Kentucky Room at the Daviess County Public Library (usually abbreviated DCPL). Sally Van Winkle Campbell was kind enough to let us use some photographs from her book *But Always Fine Bourbon: Pappy Van Winkle and the Story of Old Fitzgerald*, and Ken Hixson provided us with information and a couple of photographs from his book *Forty Miles, Forty Bridges: The Story of the Frankfort & Cincinnati Railroad*.

We would also like to thank Steve and Leslie Spears, Virgil McClain, the Haviland family, Peggy Carter, Anne Griswold, Bill Rodgers, and the Hopewell Museum.

Other titles by the Scotts available from Arcadia Publishing:

Bourbon County: 1860–1940
Paris and Bourbon County
The Kentucky Bourbon Trail (Revised Edition)
Keeneland Race Course
Kentucky's Horse-Drawn Era

INTRODUCTION

When contemplating a title for our new book about the history of bourbon distilleries in Kentucky, we first considered "Lost" as too specific. We didn't want our readers to think that the distilleries we included were totally forgotten or even somehow misplaced. But by using the term "lost" more loosely to include historic distilleries, distillers, and brands that do not exist in the same form today as they did in the past, we feel comfortable using that term for the material we have included in this book.

One of the research tools that we used when writing this book was a large poster from the Oscar Getz Museum of Whiskey History titled "History of Kentucky Distilleries." In small print, it lists 156 Kentucky distilleries with other pertinent facts, including the opening date, closing date, and the reason that the distillery closed. One of the most common reasons (for 53 distilleries) was "Lost to Prohibition." Many of those distilleries are included in this book.

In the 1800s and early 1900s, whiskey distilling in Kentucky was not for the faint of heart. Huge amounts of money had to be spent upfront on constructing a distillery, warehouses, and often an adjoining cooperage; purchasing thousands of bushels of grains and paying distillery workers to make the bourbon or rye and then move it all to the warehouses. After the bourbon was finally safely (and expensively) sitting in the warehouses, distillery owners had to wait years before any of the bourbon or rye could be sold.

Therefore, bankruptcies were commonplace, and the ownership of distilleries changed often. There were also booms and busts in the sales of bourbon, onerous taxes to be paid, restrictions on the sale of alcohol in various jurisdictions in the state and throughout the country, and national restrictions due to World War I. When one considers all the possible problems, it is a wonder that anyone stayed in the business at all.

Then came national Prohibition in 1920—a truly blighting occurrence for the distilleries in Kentucky and the thousands of jobs they provided. It was equally a catastrophe for all the farmers who depended on the distilleries to buy millions of bushels of their crops each year. In December 1933, when Prohibition was finally over, the distillery business in Kentucky came back with a "boom." However, that enthusiasm was short-lived, and many of the distilleries that had reopened in 1934 closed for good beginning in the 1950s.

This book is not intended to be a complete history of the bourbon distilling industry in Kentucky. For one thing, there is no room in the 127 pages of this book to do a comprehensive overview. Secondly, we can only write about distilleries that we have images of—a small percentage of the hundreds of distilleries that have existed in the state for more than 250 years.

That meant many distilleries could not be incorporated into this book. That included one of our favorites, W.H. Myer's Lickskillet Distillery in Warren County, about 10 miles from Bowling Green. It was one of the smallest distilleries on the 1894 Sanborn map since its capacity was only 7.5 bushels a day. That was tiny compared to most distilleries that mashed several hundred bushels a day, with a few reaching 1,000 or more bushels per day.

Today, bourbon in America—and especially in Kentucky—represents more than an alcoholic beverage, but for many, a lifestyle. Magazines like the *Bourbon Review* and others feature articles on food, fashion, cigars, travel, books, gardening, bourbon-related tours, entertainment, and distilling industry news. These things were not imagined to be a part of the "bourbon experience" a generation or two ago.

Our *Kentucky's Lost Bourbon Distilleries* is not about any of those things. It is a portrayal of the early bourbon distillery business in Kentucky, primarily before and shortly after Prohibition, using historical images from public and family archives in Kentucky.

A short explanation of what makes a whiskey, a bourbon, is in order: bourbon is a type of barrel-aged American whiskey distilled primarily from corn. The recipe, called a "mash bill," besides containing at least 51 percent ground corn, also contains a combination of other grains. The grain is ground and mixed with water. In order to make "sour mash" bourbon, a small portion of the previous batch, called the set-back, is added to the current batch to ensure a consistent taste across batches. Yeast is the final addition before the mash is fermented. After distillation is finished, the new whiskey must be aged in new, white-oak barrels.

Statistics compiled by the Kentucky Distillers' Association illustrate the importance of bourbon making in the state: "As of 2020, approximately 95% of all bourbon is produced in Kentucky. As of 2020, there were 68 whiskey distilleries in Kentucky, this was up 250 percent in the past ten years. Currently, the state has more than 8.1 million barrels of bourbon in warehouses all around the Commonwealth aging—a number that greatly exceeds the state's population of about 4.3 million."

The group estimates that the distilling industry today brings more than $9 billion each year into the Kentucky economy, sustains more than 22,500 jobs with an annual payroll topping $1.2 billion a year, and draws millions of affluent tourists from around the world to the Kentucky Bourbon Trail® experience.

A key export, bourbon distilling has the state's highest job spin-off factor among top manufacturers; buys at least 17 million bushels of corn and other grains every year, mostly from Kentucky farm families; and is currently investing more than $5.2 billion in new stills, warehouses, bottling lines, tourism experiences, and more.

That is today, but this book will look at what laid the foundation for such a successful industry and how Prohibition and the Great Depression almost killed it.

One

THE BIRTH OF BOURBON

KENTUCKY STATE FAIR, 1907. Kentucky farmers showed off the wide variety of grains they grew in this photograph taken at the 1907 Kentucky State Fair. Millions of bushels of corn, wheat, barley, and rye ended up every year in bourbon made in distilleries across the state until Prohibition closed almost all in 1920. This market never recovered when many distilleries did not reopen and were "lost" when Prohibition ended in 1933. (Glass Plate Negative Collection, UKSC.)

CABIN AND CORN PATCH. Even though this photograph was taken much later, it illustrates what early Kentucky settlers had to do to get title to the land. At that point, Kentucky was part of Virginia, and Virginia law specified that settlers had to build a log cabin and plant a required number of acres of corn to get the all-important deed. (Clay Lancaster Collection, UKSC.)

GOOD WATER IS ESSENTIAL. The water used by many distilleries is naturally filtered through layers of limestone that lie under much of Kentucky. The water is iron-free and rich in magnesium and calcium, making it among the sweetest in the world. This combination of minerals also makes the enzymes produced during mashing more efficient. An abundant and consistent supply of water is necessary for all distilleries. (Louis Nollau Collection, UKSC.)

IT BEGAN WITH THE CORN. The unique taste of bourbon whiskey began with the predominance of corn as an agricultural crop in early Kentucky. Making whiskey was nothing new to many of the first settlers who arrived in the state. The difference in the whiskey they made in Kentucky compared to what they had been distilling in other states was that corn now made up the bulk of the mash bill. In fact, bourbon has been called "the best thing that ever happened to corn," and certainly millions of bushels of corn have made their way into America's "native" liquor. Corn is a product of the New World and it contributes a lot of starch, which is converted to alcohol, and taste to the finished product. A mash bill of at least 51 percent corn is one of the requirements that are mandatory for a whiskey to be labeled as bourbon, according to a law passed in 1964. This photograph illustrates just how big the Kentucky corn crop grew around 1918. (Louis Nollau Collection, UKSC.)

WHEAT WAS OFTEN ADDED. Although the majority of the mash that is the first step in distilling bourbon is made up of corn, the rest of the mash is made from other grains, including wheat and malted barley. This photograph shows two wheat reaping machines, pulled by teams of three mules, harvesting the wheat in a central Kentucky field in the early 1900s. (Glass Plate Negative Collection, UKSC.)

RYE WAS POPULAR. Sour mash rye whiskey was made by many distilleries around the state. Some distilleries made both rye and bourbon whiskies, many produced only sour mash or sweet mash bourbon, and a few produced only rye whiskey. There were hundreds of bourbon and rye whiskeys produced—something for every taste. This photograph of a rye plot in Kentucky was taken in 1908. (Agricultural Experiment Station Photograph Collection, UKSC.)

Form 12

FORM OF DISTILLERS'

[Every distiller is required to enter daily all the transactions comprised under the headings in this book,

RECORD of Materials purchased and Repairs made in Distillery No. _111_ carried on by _H. McKenna Inc_

		KIND of	QUANTITY							FUEL PURCHASED	
DATE 1935		Materials Purchased	Lbs.	Bush.	Galls.	From Whom Purchased	Conveyed to Distillery by	Cost		Description	Quantity
May	1	Corn	8400 x	150		S Zorn & Co	Truck	150	56	✓ ✓	
"	1	"	8400	150		"	Duplicated			✓	
"	3	"	8400 x	150		"	"	148	88	✓ ✓	
"	4	Malt	40800	1200		Kurth Malting Co	R.R. + Truck	168	00		
"	7	Rye	8400	150		S Zorn & Co	Truck	106	31	✓ ✓	
"	8	Corn	8400 x	150		Do	"	149	44	✓ ✓	
"	8	Corn	8400 x	150		Do	"	149	44	✓ ✓	
"	9	Corn	16800 x	300		Do	"	300	75	✓ ✓	
"	10	Corn	16800 x	300		Do	"	295	13	✓ ✓	
"	16	Rye	16800 x	300		Do	"	202	13	✓ ✓	
"	17	Corn	8400 x	150		Do	"	52 63 / 294 75		✓ ✓	
"	17	"	8400 x	150		Do	"	52 63			
"	20	"	8400 x	150		Do	"	148 31		✓ ✓	
"	21	"	8400 x	150		Do	"				
"	21	"	8400 x	150		Do	"	293 63		✓ ✓	
"	22	"	8400 x	150		Do	"				
"	22	"	8400 x	150		Do	"	292 88		✓ ✓	
"	23	"	8400 x	150		Do	"	147 75		✓ ✓	
"	24	"	16800 x	300		Do	"	290 25		✓ ✓	
"	27	Rye	16800 x	300		Do	"	192 75		✓ ✓	
"	28	Corn	16800 x	300		Do	"	287 75		✓ ✓	
"	29	"	8400 x	150		Do	"	142 88		✓ ✓	
"	31	"	8400 x	150		Do	"	142 88 / 5414 49		✓	
"	"	"		8450		Do					
	C	8400		154		on hand end season					
	R	750		100							
	M	1700		0							
		8450									

McKenna Distillery's Busy May. This form lists all the materials purchased by the H. McKenna Distillery in May 1935. The distillery, located near Fairfield, purchased corn, malt, and rye. The largest single purchase was malt, which was purchased from Kurth Malting Co. The company had plants in several cities in the Midwest, including Milwaukee and Minneapolis. The malt was the only bourbon whiskey ingredient included on the form that was conveyed to the distillery by train. Using malt helps provide the enzymes that are needed during the mashing process when water and heat are added to the grain combination to help break down the starches in the grains to sugars. The distillery purchased more bushels of corn than any other ingredient, which makes sense since bourbon has to be made using a mash bill of at least 51 percent corn. (Marcella McKenna Collection, UKSC.)

13

SOME BARRELS TRAVELED IN WAGONS. This photograph was probably taken around the turn of the century, judging by the utility posts in the background. Barrels of bourbon traveled in wagons pulled by a variety of animals including horses, mules, and in this photograph, oxen. The barrels were likely either being transported from a distillery to a warehouse or from a warehouse to a consumer in town. (Louis Nollau Collection, UKSC.)

A TRAILBLAZING BOURBON. This label for Old Boone Kentucky Straight Bourbon Whiskey says that it is "The pioneer of Kentucky Bourbons. Distilled since 1780 from the finest grains, using Kentucky's famous limestone water." The bourbon, named after famed explorer, pioneer, and trailblazer Daniel Boone, was produced by the Old Boone Distillery in Meadowlawn, Kentucky. After a fire and a boiler explosion, the distillery closed in 1977. (Authors' collection.)

SHIPPED UP OR DOWN THE RIVER. As Central Kentucky farmer-distillers began to produce more than they could use or sell locally, they began searching for new outlets for their product. One mode of transportation was shipping barrels down the Ohio River from the closest port of Maysville. These two postcards show two views of the small port town of Maysville, originally called Limestone, from a hill overlooking the town and the river as well as a steamboat on the Ohio River. The town was then in "Old Bourbon County," because the original boundaries of Bourbon County included it. Consequently, barrels shipped from there were most likely labeled "old Bourbon," and consumers at the other end began to call the corn-based whiskey "bourbon." (Both, Postcard Collection, UKSC.)

ONE OF THE FIRST DISTILLERS. Jacob Spears moved to Kentucky in the 1780s and started distilling corn-based whiskey, which eventually bore the name of his home county of Bourbon. He was certainly one of the first bourbon distillers although no one can prove who was first. Local legends recount stories of Spears' sons shepherding loads of their barreled bourbon down the river to New Orleans on flatboats. (Steve Spears.)

EARLY STONE BOURBON WAREHOUSE. This sturdy structure still standing in Bourbon County is a very early example of a building used to store bourbon. It was built for early bourbon maker Jacob Spears and his family, along with Spears' nearby home, Stone Castle. A historical marker near the site states that the buildings and the nearby stone springhouse comprise "the most complete distiller's complex in existence today." (Carolyn Woolsey Collection, UKSC.)

SCOTT COUNTY LANDMARK. The privately funded marker at the top right says that Rev. Elijah Craig, a Baptist minister, was the first man to make bourbon whiskey and that he also developed "the first sour mash process in the production of bourbon." There were probably several early distillers who made bourbon, but the fact that Reverend Craig was a Baptist minister makes an amusing story and is an often-repeated "legend." (Postcard Collection, UKSC.)

BAPTIST PREACHER AND DISTILLER. Rev. Elijah Craig is one of the candidates for the title "Father of Bourbon." Reverend Craig was a Baptist minister who moved to Kentucky in search of religious freedom in 1781. He settled in what is now Scott County, Kentucky, which at that point was part of Fayette County, Virginia, before Kentucky became a state. He opened a distillery in the late 1780s. (Heaven Hill Distillery.)

One theory
on how bourbon whiskey
got its now-famous name
is that someone living
in Bourbon County was
the first to make what
is now recognized as
bourbon. Besides Jacob
Spears, another man
mentioned as possibly the
first to make bourbon
is Daniel Shawhan.
Both the Spears and
Shawhan families lived
and made whiskey
in Bourbon County
beginning in the 1780s.
(Authors' collection.)

WAS JOHN RITCHIE THE FIRST?
This page is from a 1901 booklet
titled *Kentucky the Beautiful,* issued
by the passenger department
of the L&N Railroad. After
mentioning people gulping
down their "half-fingers of
old Bourbon," it touts John
Ritchie as "the first distiller of
that whisky which has made
Kentucky famous." Ritchie's
"primitive plant" was located
near Bardstown, according
to the booklet. (UKSC.)

LOUISVILLE & NASHVILLE R. R.

ORIGINAL OLD BOURBON DISTILLERY—MODERN PLANTS OF
THE STATE—THROUGH THE MOONSHINERS' COUNTRY.

ERE'S to the health of John Ritchie." If such
a toast should be offered anywhere in Louisville during a national gathering the crowd
would think the one who held the glass aloft had
suddenly gone wrong and would discourteously
gulp down their half-fingers of old Bourbon
before wondering aloud, "Who in thunder is
Ritchie?"

The drink they had just taken could have
answered the question. John Ritchie was the
first distiller of that whisky which has made
Kentucky famous. Near Bardstown, a two hours' ride on
the Louisville & Nashville Railroad from Louisville, are yet
to be seen the ruins of this primitive plant, the original sour-
mash house of the Bluegrass State, or, for that matter, of
America.

It was in the early days of the last century that Ritchie,
a native of Scotland, built this distillery and made the first
gallon of old Bourbon. This little still-house was eighteen
feet square, with puncheon floor. In this structure the
meal was scalded and put through the necessary fermentation, after which the beer was carried over to the still in
buckets and the process of distillation completed. The old
furnace on which stood the copper worm still stands, the
only monument to Ritchie's memory. The **Sack of Corn**
water used by this pioneer whisky-maker **Legal Tender**
came from a never-failing spring of ice- **for Whisky**
cold water near the distillery. By the process used by Ritchie
he could only get a yield of one gallon of whisky to each

39

18

[License to work a Still for distilling Spirits from Domestic Materials.]

No.

WHEREAS *William Crow* of the of
in the County of *Lincoln* in the *State*
Collection District of *Kentucky* possessor of a Still of the capacity of *one*
Gallons, including the head thereof, at this time erected
and intended to be used in the of in the County of
Lincoln in the District aforesaid, and owned by *the said William*
Crow of in the County of *Lincoln*
and District aforesaid, hath duly applied for a License to distil Spirits from Domestic Materials,
during the term of three months, to commence on the *first* day of *January* 1814, and to end
on the *first* day of *April* 1814:

NOW KNOW YE, That the said *William Crow* is hereby licensed to work and
employ the said Still in distilling Spirits from DOMESTIC MATERIALS, for the said term of THREE MONTHS, as above
defined, in conformity with an Act of Congress, passed the 24th day of July, 1813.

Countersigned at *Stanford* in the Collec-
tion District aforesaid, this *twenty ninth* day of
Decr 18*13*
Commissioner of the Revenue.

*Collector of the Revenue for the Sixth Collec*tion
District of *Kentucky*

EARLY LICENSE. This license was issued in Lincoln County in 1813. It gave William Crow "license to work a Still for distilling spirits." Crow lived in a region that has been located in three different counties through the years. As the state grew and the larger counties were divided, Crow's very early stone house was located, at one time, in Lincoln, Mercer, and Boyle Counties. (Joseph Seagram & Sons Photographs, UKSC.)

COOPERAGE IN BOONE COUNTY. The early 1800s saw the ever-increasing production of bourbon (and rye) whiskey as distilling became an industry that had far outgrown the confines of a family farm. As shown in this photograph of an early cooperage at the Boone County Distillery, making barrels was an indispensable craft essential to keep up with the amount of liquor that needed to be aged in barrels. (Boone County Library.)

KENTUCKY'S FIRST COMMERCIAL DISTILLER. Evan Williams is generally recognized as the first commercial distiller in the state. He operated his distillery, beginning in 1783, in a riverfront location in Louisville. According to a historical marker recognizing Williams, his large-scale distillery was situated on the banks of the Ohio River, making it convenient to ship flat-boat loads of the corn-based bourbon from Kentucky to points north and south. (Heaven Hill Distillery.)

BOURBON IN SCHNAPPS BOTTLES? That is what Udolpho Wolfe was promising in this 1863 advertisement that ran in New York City's *Sunday Dispatch.* It is good to know that he thought the bourbon, produced in the Kentucky county of that name, could be relied on by the medical profession. He does not specify what the elixir can cure, but it would not take "a spoonful of sugar" to make that medicine go down. (Library of Congress.)

4

Business World.

PURE BOURBON WHISKEY.

TO THE CITIZENS OF NEW YORK.

For some time past, I have been solicited by the Medical Faculty of this city to add to my "Schiedam Aromatic Schnapps" business, the bottling of PURE BOURBON WHISKEY, which could be relied on by the medical profession. I would have acceded to their request some time since, but found it difficult to procure a pure article. After considerable difficulty and delay, I have arranged with two distillers in Bourbon county for a regular supply. I have also located an agent in Louisville, Ky., for the purchase of BOURBON WHISKEY direct from the distillers, when offered for sale in that market.

The Whiskey will be put up in my Schnapps bottles, and packed in cases of one dozen each, with a fac-simile of my signature on the label.

For sale by all Grocers, Druggists, and Apothecaries.

I remain, yours, respectfully,

UDOLPHO WOLFE,

No. 22 Beaver street.

NEW YORK, February 14, 1863.

$I\Omega\Delta H\Sigma.$

Two

EARLY BOURBON
DISTILLERIES

MAKING BOURBON IN MARION COUNTY. Richard Cummins was involved with several distilleries in Nelson County, including the Coon Hollow Distillery, after immigrating from Ireland in 1848. He purchased the Ballard & Lancaster Distillery at Loretto in Marion County in 1885 and renamed it the R. Cummins & Co. Distillery. Cummins is pictured here (second from left on the platform) with his distillery crew in 1890. (Oscar Getz Museum of Whiskey History.)

TOO COLD FOR DISTILLING. This 1915 photograph of the A. Keller Distillery in Harrison County illustrates why bourbon could only be distilled during the warmer months in Kentucky. Many distilleries used water from nearby rivers, streams, ponds, or springs to make their products, all of which could freeze in the winter. Icicles can be seen descending from the eaves of the closest buildings. (The Haviland family.)

A DAY OUT AT KELLER DISTILLERY. These girls were enjoying the sunshine at the Keller Distillery before it was closed by Prohibition in 1920. The girl on the left was probably part of a school group that was featured in other photographs of that day. The girl on the right is wearing what looks like the clothing worn by the women and girls who bottled the bourbon. (Peggy Carter.)

A. KELLER DISTILLERY   CYNTHIANA, KY.

POSTCARD VIEW OF KELLER DISTILLERY. The Keller Distillery, pictured here, was one of several located in Harrison County in the area that was once part of Bourbon County. At one time, Harrison County was reportedly home to 30 distilleries—more than most of the counties in the state. This distillery was built in 1840 by Abraham Keller, closed because of Prohibition in 1920, and never reopened. (Postcard Collection, UKSC.)

PRODUCED SEVERAL TYPES OF WHISKEY. As seen in this billhead dated April 2, 1879, the firm of Megibben, Bramble & Co. was the successor of the firm of T.J. Megibben & Bro. They produced "Pure Bourbon, Rye & Wheat Whiskies," something for every taste, at the Excelsior Distillery located at Lair's Station in Harrison County. The distillery ran six months of the year and produced 8,000 barrels annually. (Denny Lipscomb.)

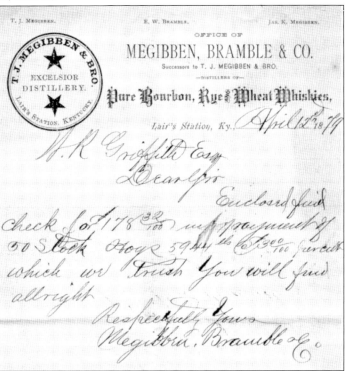

KENTUCKY VERSION OF MONTICELLO. Thomas Jefferson "T.J." Megibben built this lovely home with 32 rooms on a hilltop near Cynthiana in 1883 at a cost of $300,000. Since his name was Thomas Jefferson Megibben, he decided to call his new home "Monticello" after the well-known Virginia home of Thomas Jefferson. The house took seven years to build, and Megibben lived in it for seven years before he died. (Anne Griswold.)

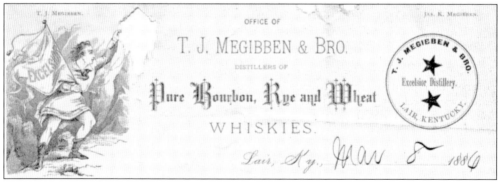

EXCELSIOR DISTILLERY'S NEW LOGO. Although some histories state that the Excelsior Distillery became the Edgewater Distillery, early Sanborn maps show both operating at the same time. One was on Woods Run and the other on the South Fork of the Licking River, both in Lair in Harrison County. Both distilleries were owned by T.J. Megibben in partnership with family members. (Denny Lipscomb.)

JULIUS KESSLER AND OLD LEWIS HUNTER DISTILLERY. By the 1894 Sanborn map, Julius Kessler & Co. owned the Old Lewis Hunter distillery in Lair, which was four miles southwest of Cynthiana in Harrison County. It was formerly the site of the R.G. Sharpe & Co. Distillery. The Old Lewis Hunter distillery was on the South Fork of the Licking River and produced sour mash rye and bourbon whiskies. According to the 1910 Sanborn map, like many distilleries of the time, there was steam heat in all the warehouses. The office and the yeast room were both heated with coal stoves. For light, they used lard oil lanterns. The facility was up-to-date for the time as it had the Grinnell auto sprinkling system installed in the distillery and boiler room. Another interesting feature was a steel water tower, 85 feet tall with a capacity of 24,000 gallons. (Joseph Seagram & Sons Photographs, UKSC.)

Kentucky and Whiskey

Among the many noteworthy achievements of Kentuckians the distilling of the finest and rarest whiskies stands out preeminent. Few of her history-making sons have done more to carry her manifold virtues broadcast than has her renowned whiskies, the most splendid alcoholic derivative of grain produced since its discovery by Alkubassen in the tenth century.

KENTUCKY QUALITY ELIMINATES DISTANCE

We Sell the Finest Kentucky Whiskies and Georgia Corn

EXPRESS PREPAID

Four Full Quarts (in glass)

ATTIC		BLUE LABEL	
Finest Kentucky Bourbon	$4.00	Pure Old Corn	$4.00
WILLOW DALE RYE		ALLAN SINCLAIRS	
Old and Fragrant	$2.85	Georgia Corn	$2.85

The Swift Creek Distilling Co.
(Incorporated)

LOUISVILLE, KY.

"If We Distill It---It's Right"

1

KENTUCKY, WHISKEY, AND SWASTIKAS? This advertisement that ran in the *Montgomery Advertiser* in May 1908 is interesting for several reasons. It is for a distillery that has not been included in the book so far; it talks about using "Georgia" corn when almost all the pre-Prohibition distilleries used home-grown Kentucky corn; and it is bordered by swastikas. This was in 1908, long before the Nazis had ruined the ancient swastika symbol by attaching it to their evil regime. The advertisement also illustrates another way that Americans in 1908 could obtain liquor: shipped directly by "express prepaid." That meant that you could visit a saloon for a drink of Kentucky whiskey, purchase it at a store (usually a drugstore), or order it shipped directly in quart bottles. This distillery was not listed by this name on either the 1894 or 1910 Sanborn maps of distilleries in the state but was possibly operating under another name. It does not sound like it was just purchasing whiskey from other distilleries and renaming it because of their slogan: "If We Distill It–It's Right." (Library of Congress.)

CEDAR BROOK DISTILLERY. William McBrayer established his distillery on Cedar Brook Run east of Lawrenceburg in 1844. Cedar Brook whiskey won a medal at the Philadelphia Centennial in 1876. The distillery was run by his family until 1899, when it was sold to Julius Kessler and Company. In 1903, the company installed the 2.5-mile water line to the Kentucky River seen at the bottom right. (Ripy family collection.)

POPULAR BOURBONS, 1909. Kentucky whiskey was a well-known and respected brand and a desired product across America by 1909 when this advertisement appeared in New York's *The Sun*, advertising W.H. McBrayer's Cedar Brook, Old Lewis Hunter Rye, and Melwood Bourbon. Melwood claimed to be "One of Kentucky's Real Bourbons," and McBrayer's Cedar Brook said it was the "World's Finest Whiskey." (Library of Congress.)

Bottled in Bond
Distillery Built in 1801
The Hannis Distilling Co., Proprietors
W. H. McBrayer's Cedar Brook
The World's Finest Whiskey
Bottled in Bond   *Known Throughout the World*
Julius Kessler & Co., Distillers

Old Lewis Hunter Rye
One of the Oldest Whiskies Produced in Kentucky
Bottled in Bond
Old Lewis Hunter Distillery, Lair, Ky.

Melwood Bourbon
One of Kentucky's Real Bourbons
Bottled in Bond

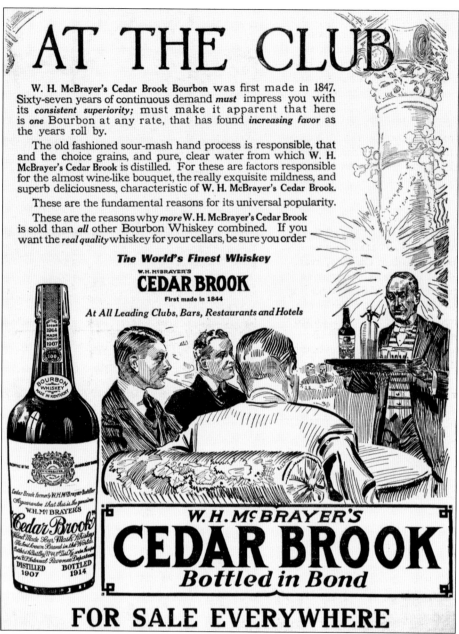

AT THE CLUB

W. H. McBrayer's Cedar Brook Bourbon was first made in 1847. Sixty-seven years of continuous demand *must* impress you with its *consistent superiority;* must make it apparent that here is *one* Bourbon at any rate, that has found *increasing favor* as the years roll by.

The old fashioned sour-mash hand process is responsible, that and the choice grains, and pure, clear water from which W. H. McBrayer's Cedar Brook is distilled. For these are factors responsible for the almost wine-like bouquet, the really exquisite mildness, and superb deliciousness, characteristic of W. H. McBrayer's Cedar Brook.

These are the fundamental reasons for its universal popularity.

These are the reasons why *more* W. H. McBrayer's Cedar Brook is sold than *all* other Bourbon Whiskey combined. If you want the *real quality* whiskey for your cellars, be sure you order

The World's Finest Whiskey

W.H. McBRAYER'S
CEDAR BROOK
First made in 1844

At All Leading Clubs, Bars, Restaurants and Hotels

W. H. McBRAYER'S
CEDAR BROOK
Bottled in Bond

FOR SALE EVERYWHERE

NATIONAL RENOWN DESERVED NATIONAL ADVERTISING. By 1914, when this large full-page advertisement appeared in the *Omaha Daily Bee*, Cedar Brook Bourbon was owned by Julius Kessler & Company, which touted the bourbon's reputation as "The World's Finest Whiskey." Their advertising proudly claimed that the sour mash process and the "choice grains, and pure, clear water from which W.H. McBrayer's Cedar Brook is distilled" was "responsible for the almost wine-like bouquet, the exquisite mildness and superb deliciousness." These attributes led to the bourbon's "universal popularity." The ad writers also claim that more Cedar Brook was sold "than all other Bourbon Whiskey combined." As with most of the distilleries at the time, Cedar Brook was shut down in 1920 due to Prohibition, but descendants of McBrayer have recently begun selling a limited edition of McBrayer Legacy Spirits based on his original recipe. (Library of Congress.)

ANDERSON COUNTY DISTILLING FAMILY.
In 1820, John Bond built a distillery on a site close to the Cedar Brook Distillery in Anderson County. His son, William F. Bond (pictured) eventually took over and formed a partnership with his brother-in-law C.C. Lillard in 1869. The distillery and name were sold to Lexington's Stoll and Company, which won the grand prize for their whiskey at the 1904 Louisiana Purchase Exposition. (Ripy family collection.)

BOND'S MILL DISTILLERY. In June 1892, the Bond & Lillard Distillery near Bond's Mill was razed by fire at an estimated loss of $10,000. According to the *New York Times*, it was not insured. The property was acquired by Stoll & Company in 1899 and successfully produced quality bourbon until Prohibition. This photograph is of the distillery building constructed after the fire. (Joseph Seagram & Sons Photographs, UKSC.)

Everyone, Including the Kids. This large group of men and three boys shows the variety of workers employed by distilleries. The men dressed in the rougher clothing were the workers who performed a variety of tasks in the distillery including unloading thousands of bushels of grains each month, moving the grain to the mash tubs and then to the fermenting containers. The African American man with the mule team was probably one of the employees who worked with the horses and mules that provided the transport. The men in front, dressed in white shirts and ties, were probably the office staff and revenue department representatives who were assigned to every distillery in Kentucky. At a guess, the man in the center with the bow tie and vest was the distillery owner. There are two boys in the first row and a well-dressed young man in a tie and vest seated on the wagon. This photograph was taken between 1894 and 1905 at the Old Prentice Distillery. (Joseph Seagram & Sons Photographs, UKSC.)

THIS DISTILLERY USED WATER POWER. This weir (or dam) behind the Bond's Mill Distillery, channeled the power of running water to the mill that provided power to the distillery. The distillery was located near Lawrenceburg in Anderson County and, according to the Lawrenceburg newspaper, was the only water-powered distillery in the country. That would have meant a considerable savings to the distillery owners. Not only did they not have to buy the coal that usually powered the boilers, but they also did not have to have workmen to transport the coal from train cars to the distillery property and then to the boiler room and other areas at the distillery where the coal was burned. This distillery changed names through the years, like many other distilleries in the state, and is currently the site of the Four Roses Distillery. (Joseph Seagram & Sons Photographs, UKSC.)

ORIGINAL O.F.C. DISTILLERY. This illustration is from an 1886 booklet titled *Compliments of E.H. Taylor & Co., Distillers, Frankfort, KY.* The booklet was aimed at the general public and "especially the whiskey trade," and expounded all the superlatives of three main distilleries owned by the E.H. Taylor & Co.: O.F.C., Carlisle, and J. Swigart Taylor. Shown is the original O.F.C. Distillery in 1869 that was torn down in 1873. (UKSC.)

SHORT-LIVED DISTILLERY. This handsome edifice was built by Col. Edmund Taylor Jr. after the earlier O.F.C. Distillery building, which the booklet described as "primitive," was torn down. Less than a decade later, the building shown was destroyed by fire which was an ever-present hazard for the industry. Note that the building was only three stories tall and is out of scale with the men and barrels shown in front of it. (UKSC.)

MASH FLOOR OF O.F.C. DISTILLERY

MASH FLOOR OF THE O.F.C. DISTILLERY. This illustration shows the mash floor at the O.F.C. Distillery in 1886. According to the booklet published that year, the grain meal is received directly from the room above where it was milled. That can be seen at far left in the illustration, where workers are collecting the correct amount of grain in a small tub to be put in one of the barrels shown. That is then combined with the heated "strained sour spent beer" at the correct temperature required for cooking the mash. After it has been mixed thoroughly by hand, the mixture remains in the barrels for 24 hours. The booklet states that "the rye and barley malt are added at the juncture most suitable for developing the spirit properties." The whole process took 96 hours and was being done continuously during the day to insure a smooth flow of the finished product. (UKSC.)

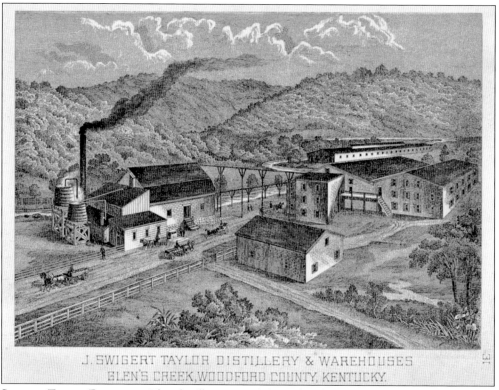

J. SWIGERT TAYLOR DISTILLERY & WAREHOUSES
GLEN'S CREEK, WOODFORD COUNTY, KENTUCKY.

SMALLER TAYLOR DISTILLERY. This distillery, named for Colonel Taylor's son Jacob Swigert Taylor was located on Glenn's Creek in Woodford County. By 1894, the distillery was the E.H. Taylor & Sons' Old Taylor Distillery. The 1886 booklet mentions that the site had been used since 1819 for distilling bourbon. Taylor's son was probably named for Phillip Swigert, Frankfort mayor for 20 years, an office also held by Colonel Taylor. (UKSC.)

Fac-Simile of Cooperage and Trade Mark Brands.

THREE PROUD BRANDS. Col. E.H. Taylor Jr. was proud of the bourbons made in the three distilleries he owned in 1886. His flagship distillery was the O.F.C. Distillery near Frankfort in Franklin County. The Carlisle Distillery was next door to the O.F.C. and the J.S. Taylor distillery was located in Woodford County. Taylor was rather obsessive about cleanliness, which is why he touted his "all-copper" distilling process. (UKSC.)

34

FRANKFORT TROLLEY STOP. This photograph shows an office building divided up between "E.H. Taylor, Jr. Co. Incorporated, Distiller" and "Geo. T. Stagg Co. Incorporated, Wholesale Liquor Dealer," according to the signs hanging over the two entrances. Stagg was a liquor distributor before he met Colonel Taylor and became his partner. The liquor business had good years and bad years and financial partnerships were sometimes a necessity. (Bill Rodgers collection.)

LOTS OF STAGS. There are several stags pictured around this office at the George Stagg Distillery in Frankfort. The man seated at the desk is probably George Stagg. Stagg was Colonel Taylor's partner until money problems forced Taylor out of the partnership. Taylor then formed the company E.H. Taylor and Sons and expanded the J. Swigert Taylor Distillery, renaming it the Old Taylor Distillery. (Bill Rodgers collection.)

WIDE-ANGLE VIEW OF MATTINGLY DISTILLERY. This distillery, listed as the B.F. Mattingly Distillery on the 1894 Sanborn map, was located in Marion County. This photograph, taken between 1903–1905, shows the employees and perhaps the owners—one mounted on horseback at the back of the standing group and one standing up in the horse-drawn buggy in the background in front of the bourbon warehouses. The distillery building with a 60-foot-tall chimney can be seen

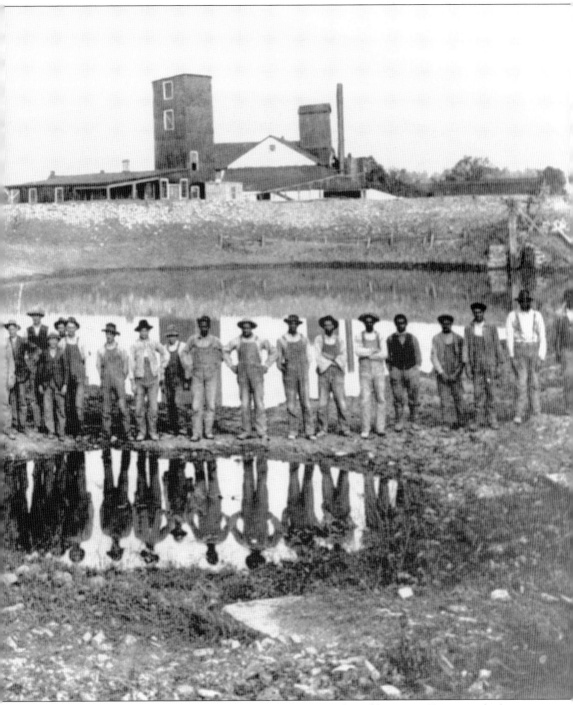

in the background on the right. The distillery was later purchased by Brown-Forman, which ran the distillery until around 1918 when they closed it due to grain rationing during World War I. In 1923, the remaining bourbon had to be moved to a Federal Concentration Warehouse due to Prohibition. The facility was shut down then and soon after was totally destroyed by fire. (Brown-Forman Archives.)

LABELING OLD CROW. These ladies are putting labels and tax stamps on bottles of Old Crow produced by the W.A. Gaines Company. Once whiskey began being sold in bottles instead of barrels, women were able to enter the workforce. During the warmer months, when bourbon was produced, many Kentucky newspapers carried periodic classified ads seeking "bottling girls" to work at various distilleries. (Oscar Getz Museum of Whiskey History.)

RISQUE 1870 LABEL. This Old Crow label has a handwritten notation that says, "Filled Jany 25th 1870," and is quite frisky for that era when the sight of a woman's ankle was enough to raise a man's blood pressure. The Old Crow Distillery was located on Glenn's Creek in Woodford County. The bourbon was very popular during the Civil War, and it was supposedly Ulysses S. Grant's favorite whiskey. (Library of Congress.)

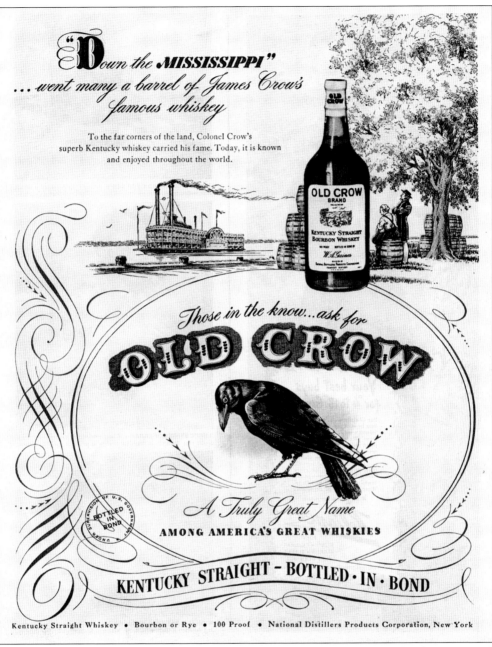

"**Down the MISSISSIPPI**"

... *went many a barrel of James Crow's famous whiskey*

To the far corners of the land, Colonel Crow's superb Kentucky whiskey carried his fame. Today, it is known and enjoyed throughout the world.

Those in the know...ask for

OLD CROW

A Truly Great Name

AMONG AMERICA'S GREAT WHISKIES

KENTUCKY STRAIGHT - BOTTLED · IN · BOND

Kentucky Straight Whiskey • Bourbon or Rye • 100 Proof • National Distillers Products Corporation, New York

IMAGINATIVE ADVERTISING. This is just one of the thousands of advertisements that have appeared touting a particular brand of whiskey as the "best ever." The first known bourbon advertisement was printed in the *Western Citizen* in Paris, Kentucky, in 1821. One thing to notice in this advertisement is that Dr. James Crow is now a colonel and "his superb Kentucky whiskey has carried his fame throughout the world." The Old Crow Distillery was heavily into marketing and the visit to the distillery by Mark Twain in the 1880s led to a flurry of advertisements. The Old Crow Distillery continued to produce bourbon under the ownership of National Distillers until the 1980s. At that time, it was purchased by the Jim Beam Brands Company, and the distillery was closed. The warehouses on the site are still used to store bourbon. (Authors' collection.)

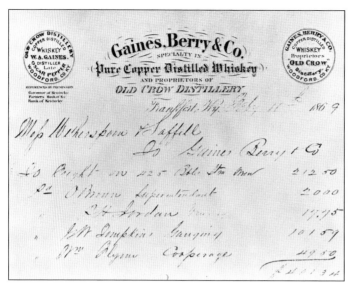

CALENDAR PHOTOGRAPH, 1894. Boone & Bros. Distillery at Gethsemane was a small distillery that only used 67 bushels of grain per day (some of the largest distilleries used 1,000 bushels or more per day). It was located on the Beech Fork and the Loretto Pike. Frank Boone is in the upper right-hand window, and Nick Boone is fourth from the right. Their brands were Boone Bros. and Old Maid. (Dixie Hibbs.)

OLD TRUMP WHISKEY ADVERTISING. This antique advertising mirror is on display at the Oscar Getz Museum. It advertises Old Trump whiskey. The name had nothing to do with a past president since it advertises a whiskey that was made in the late 1800s at the Head and Beam Distillery in Nelson County. The distillery was also run as G. and B. Gerdes Mountain Lilly Distillery. (Oscar Getz Museum of Whiskey History.)

EARLY OLD PRENTICE DISTILLERY. Around 1905, J.T.S. Brown and Sons, makers of Old Prentice and other brands, acquired this large facility on the banks of the Salt River. This photograph shows the "barrel track" that distillery workers used to roll barrels full of bourbon from the distillery to the seven-story warehouse seen in the background. The Old Prentice brand had been around since 1855. (Joseph Seagram & Sons Photographs, UKSC.)

LABEL REVEALS BARTON DISTILLING COMPANY'S ROOTS. This label for Bourbon County brand Kentucky Straight Bourbon Whiskey shows it was bottled by the Barton Distilling Company in Bardstown, which is in Nelson County. However, that distillery was one of three owned at one time by Joshua Barton. He was a lifelong resident of Millersburg in Bourbon County, and one of his distilleries was located there, which explains the name. (Authors' collection.)

GRAND DAD KNOWS BEST. The image of R.B. Hayden in this advertisement shows him at a much younger age than the bust being carved in the advertisement on the facing page. But whatever age he is shown at, he is always credited with being the originator of Old Grand Dad, a handmade, sour mash bourbon. The Hayden family's first distillery was built in 1840 in Nelson County. (Library of Congress.)

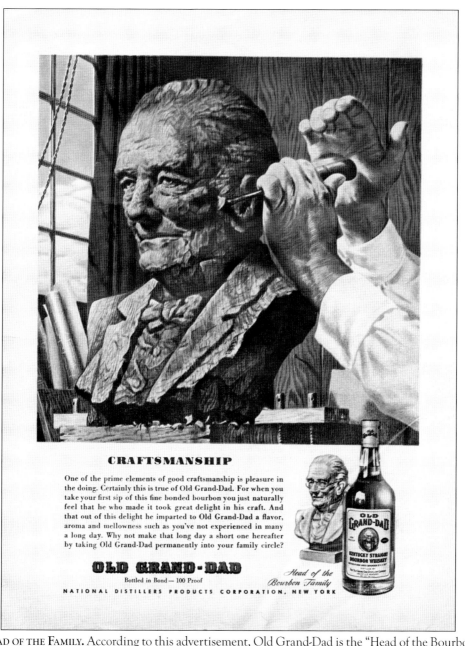

CRAFTSMANSHIP

One of the prime elements of good craftsmanship is pleasure in the doing. Certainly this is true of Old Grand-Dad. For when you take your first sip of this fine bonded bourbon you just naturally feel that he who made it took great delight in his craft. And that out of this delight he imparted to Old Grand-Dad a flavor, aroma and mellowness such as you've not experienced in many a long day. Why not make that long day a short one hereafter by taking Old Grand-Dad permanently into your family circle?

OLD GRAND-DAD
Bottled in Bond — 100 Proof
NATIONAL DISTILLERS PRODUCTS CORPORATION, NEW YORK

Head of the Bourbon Family

HEAD OF THE FAMILY. According to this advertisement, Old Grand-Dad is the "Head of the Bourbon Family." The brand began in the 1880s and has been produced at several distilleries, most of them no longer in business, including the one named after it in Frankfort. The bust being carved in the advertisement is of Basil Hayden, the originator of the recipe for Old Grand-Dad (note the name has gained a hyphen since the earlier advertisement on the facing page), which contains more rye than many bourbon whiskies. The brand's label used a drawing of Basil Hayden Sr. until 1939, when National Distillers, who owned the brand at that time, commissioned the bust of the famous grandfather that can be seen in this advertisement. The advertisement suggests bourbon drinkers should improve their lives by "taking Old Grand-Dad permanently into your family circle." (Authors' collection.)

Four Oaks Distilling Co.
402-404 North 26th Street
Birmingham, Ala.

— We Carry the Largest Line of —

Whiskies, Imported Wines and Beers In the South

We Beg to Submit the Following Brands For Your Consideration

Monticello Special Reserve	Old Forester	Peach Brandy
T. B. Ripy, 21 years old	Murray Hill	Gordon Dry Gin
Jas. E. Pepper, 21 years old	Jefferson Club	Carolina Belle
Old Crow	Paul Jones	Virginia Dare
Hermitage	Mellwood	Chrystallized Rock and Rye
Mt. Vernon	Budweiser Whiskey	Chrystallized Peach and
Four Roses	Woodford Club	Honey
Lewis '66	Our 500 Per Cent Straight	Sloe Gin
I. W. Harper	Old Bud	Don Carlos Sherry
Guckenheimer	Bank Note	Nieporto Port
Yellowstone	Rose Valley	Black and White Scotch
Creme de la Creme	Muscogee Club	Slator's V. O. P. Scotch
Cedar Brook	Trimble Springs	Shelham's Scotch
O. F. C.	Old Wakeman	Garn Kirk Scotch
Old Overholt	Old Joe Gideon	Usher's Scotch
Old Jordan	Dixon Club	Dewar's Scotch
Green River	Merry Land	Bushmill's Irish
T. W. Samuels	Budweiser Rye	Jameson's Irish
Cascade	Forefather	H. & U. Tom Gin
Old Oscar Pepper	Purity	H. & U. Dry Gin
Greenbriar	Chester Corn	Holland Gin
Jefferson	Old Town Corn	Martexa Gin
Old Ripy	Phosphate Gin	Aionyzoe Brandy
Deep Springs	100 Per Cent Straight Gin	French Vermuth
Peter Cooper	Sherwood	Italian Vermuth
Royal Worcester	Cream of Kentucky	Kummel
Hudson	Jim Dandy Gin	Creme-de-Menthe
Echo Springs	Railroad Rye	Curacao
Old Quaker	Magic City	Creme-de-Cacao
Lewis Hunter	Jackson Club	Annisette
J. H. Cutter	Uncle George	Maraschino
Old Senator	Shaw's Malt	**BEERS**
T. B. Ripy, 14 years old	Duffy's Malt	New York and Brooklyn
Belle of Nelson, 10 years old	McKenzie Malt	Monumental
Mudlick	Felton Old Rum	Perfect Brew
Hainer's Monogram	(Bottled in Bond)	Frank Fehr
Little Whiskey	Queensdale Gin	Budweiser
Old Hancock	Apple Brandy	Schlitz
		Peel, real German Lager

High Class Goods and Right Prices

KENTUCKY DISTILLERIES WIDELY KNOWN. This large advertisement listing bourbons and ryes, among other liquors, is from the May 12, 1912, issue of the *Birmingham Age-Herald*. The list includes several of the distilleries featured in this book: T.B. Ripy, Jas. E. Pepper, Old Crow, O.F.C., Old Oscar Pepper, and Lewis Hunter. Receiving top billing are Monticello Special Reserve, made in Harrison County; T.B. Ripy, 21 years old, made in Anderson County; and Jas. E. Pepper, 21 years old, made in Fayette County. The two bourbons listed as 21 years old would have been distilled in 1891. There are also a couple of brands listed that are less well-known, such as Mudlick Whiskey and Railroad Rye. Other unusual listings are for Budweiser Whiskey and Budweiser Rye, in addition to the Budweiser beer entry. The products of Kentucky distilleries, large and small, were popular across the country before Prohibition. (Library of Congress.)

BARDSTOWN DISTILLERY, ESTABLISHED IN 1876. The Mattingly & Moore Distillery was located one mile southwest of Bardstown. One of the bourbons distilled there for a time was "Belle of Nelson." It was probably named for the filly by that name who won the 1877 Kentucky Oaks and was owned by John Mattingly. By 1894, it was shown as the Mattingly & Moore–Simms & Edelen Distillery. (Dixie Hibbs.)

DISTILLERY'S HANDSOME LETTERHEAD. This nicely designed letterhead for the Mattingly & Moore Distillery Co. hits all the high spots, emphasizing "Hand Made" and "Sour Mash" but making sure that the word "Whiskey" was the most prominent. There is an unusual crescent moon and star motif in the center. B.F. Mattingly is shown as president, T.S. Moore as secretary and treasurer, and R. Cummins as superintendent. (Dixie Hibbs.)

MAKING MONEY FROM DISTILLERY BY-PRODUCT. This Glenmore Distilleries Company advertisement that ran in the 1916 *Hartford Herald* extolls the virtues of raising hogs. The top photograph shows horse-drawn wagons lined up waiting to "be filled with distillers' liquid feed" on the morning of April 1, 1916. The distillery sold 1,250 barrels of feed during that day, which was "about an average daily rate." The huge distilleries that used more than 1,000 bushels of grains in a day were faced with a dilemma. Although some of the spent grain mash could be sold to individual cattle and hog farmers in bulk and fed to livestock penned on the distillery grounds, that could only get rid of so much. Some distilleries dried and bagged their used "slops," but Glenmore had come up with a better plan. Selling the "liquid feed" directly to the hog farmers allowed them to skip the drying process and also moved the material off the distillery property since feeding hogs and cattle on-site was a smelly business that produced tons of manure that had to be disposed of. (Library of Congress.)

BOLDRICK AND CALLAGHAN DISTILLERY. Richard Wathen operated a distillery on the Rolling Fork River in Marion County from 1852 to 1875. The facility was sold to Ralph Spalding, who changed the name to Belle of Marion Distillery. It soon became Boldrick and Callaghan, owned by George Boldrick and Frank Callaghan. The distillery produced handmade sour mash bourbon and rye right up to Prohibition. This 1885 photograph shows the distillery crew with a wagon full of their product. They are rather well-dressed compared to some of the other crews pictured in this book. An interesting feature at the top left is a very steep barrel roll. According to the 1894 Sanborn map, the warehouse was located 45 feet above the distillery on top of what the map describes as a "steep hillside." It is hard to picture barrels going up or down, but they must have made it work. The distillery reopened after Prohibition but closed for good in 1936. (Oscar Getz Museum of Whiskey History.)

BOURBON MADE IN BOURBON COUNTY. The Peacock Distillery was located in Kiserton, about three miles north of Paris on Stoner Creek. It was one of several distilleries in the county that lent its name to corn-based whiskey before Prohibition. The distillery changed hands several times in the 1890s but was still in operation in 1910 when it was the "Peacock Distilling Co., Inc. also run as F.P. Thomas Distillery," according to the Sanborn map. (Hopewell Museum.)

PEACOCK DISTILLERY CREW. The tool the man astride the barrel (third from left) is holding is called a whiskey thief and was used to remove a small amount of bourbon while it was aging in the barrel to be tasted. At far right is R.D. Grant, one of a handful of African Americans employed by the state revenue department. The department assigned men to every distillery to ensure that taxes were paid. (Hopewell Museum.)

THE PEACOCK WHISKEY CONTAINED IN THIS BOTTLE
WAS DISTILLED, MATURED AND BOTTLED IN BOND BY
PEACOCK DISTILLERY COMPANY
REGISTERED DISTILLERY No.10. 7TH DISTRICT
PARIS, BOURBON CO. KENTUCKY, U.S.A.
UNDER THE DIRECT SUPERVISION OF THE
UNITED STATES INTERNAL REVENUE DEPARTMENT

NOT NBC—PEACOCK DISTILLERY. Long before television and the NBC network were thought of, the peacock was the proud symbol of a famous Bourbon County distillery. The Peacock Distillery was located on the banks of Stoner Creek. Behind the peacock on this label, men in a boat on the creek can be seen, as can the distillery buildings in the background. Like many distilleries, it underwent numerous changes in ownership and in the 1890s, it was supposedly one of many distilleries purchased by the Whiskey Trust. One of the distillery's outstanding features was a whiskey pipe that stretched 745 feet from the distillery to the front portion of one of the bonded warehouses that was portioned off to contain the cistern room, the government office where all the tax paperwork was done and a "branding and barrel shed" with an attached branding furnace. Outside of Kentucky Owl made at the C.M. Dedman Distillery in Oregon, Kentucky, and Old Crow, possibly the only other bourbons named for birds were Bourbon County's Peacock and Chicken Cock bourbons. (Authors' collection.)

DISTILLERY COMPLEX OUTSIDE PARIS. This photograph shows the Paris Distilling Co., formerly the Clay & Buckner Distillery, on the North Middletown Pike just outside the Paris city limits. The distillery was also known as the Sam Clay Distillery for the brand of whiskey it produced. When Prohibition became law in 1920, the facility was converted to a tobacco warehouse and tobacco redrying plant. (Hopewell Museum.)

PARIS SALOON FEATURED LOCAL BRANDS. The medicinal value of Duffy's Pure Malt Whiskey takes up most of this 1906 advertisement in the *Bourbon News* for L. Saloshin's Saloon in Paris. The bottom portion of the ad features several Bourbon County and Harrison County brands, including Old Van Hook, Sam Clay, Poindexter, and Chicken Cock (in bond). Mellwood Bourbon is also listed. The Mellwood Distillery was located in Jefferson County. (Library of Congress.)

ROLL OUT THE BARRELS. The men pictured here are either picking up or delivering barrels of Bourbon County whiskey during the 1880s. During that time, bourbon, tobacco, and bluegrass seed warehouses were scattered across the county and there were seven operating distilleries in the county. The last closed for good at the beginning of Prohibition. However, despite rumors to the contrary, Bourbon County has never been dry. (Hopewell Museum.)

CHICKEN COCK DISTILLERY. Located just a quarter mile northeast of the Bourbon County Courthouse, it was built in 1856 by James Miller, who started making a premium, well-aged, sour mash bourbon. Just a few years after Chicken Cock's founding, Miller passed away and was followed by a man named George G. White. It was used as a bluegrass seed cleaning facility after Prohibition, and it burned in 1961. (Hopewell Museum.)

ADVERTISEMENT FOR SALT RIVER BOURBON, 1860. This advertisement appeared in the *Daily Gate City* in 1860, making it one of the earliest display advertisements for bourbon that we saw. This newspaper was located in Keokuk, Iowa, and the same ad also ran in the *Idaho World* around the same time. S.T. Suit claims that his Salt River Bourbon Whiskey Distillery opened in 1839, and in another ad of the same vintage, he also claimed that the distillery, located in Louisville, was "the oldest in Kentucky." That claim was fairly common during this era and made by a number of distilleries. Suit's bourbon was also highlighted in an advertisement that appealed to chemists who filled prescriptions for "medicinal" whiskey at the time. The ads offered $500 to any chemist who could find anything other than "pure, genuine, unadulterated Bourbon" in his Salt River liquor. That was quite a princely sum in the 1860s. (Library of Congress.)

HEADING HOME FROM DISTILLERY. Several of these ladies are carrying small baskets which probably carried their lunch but since they are also all wearing hats or bonnets of some type, they are most likely on their way home. Several of their male coworkers can be seen in the background. Bottling was the one job at distilleries that was traditionally done mostly by women. They were always assisted by men or boys who could move the full barrels of bourbon into the bottling house or room and then move the full cases out to be shipped—usually by rail—to their final destination. The empty barrels also had to be disposed of. This photograph was taken at the J.B. Dant Distillery in Gethsemane, located about 18 miles west of Lebanon. They produced Yellowstone Bourbon, which was said to have been named after the national park, which opened in 1872. (Dixie Hibbs and Oscar Getz Museum of Whiskey History.)

THE MCKENNA DISTILLERY. This is a very early photograph of the McKenna Distillery located in Fairfield in Nelson County. The distillery was founded in 1858 by Henry McKenna. This photograph shows a stagecoach pulled by four horses and other horses and buggies in front of the entrance along with employees. The sign over the door says "Nelson County Sour Mash Whiskey." (Joseph Seagram and Sons Photographs, UKSC.)

MCKENNA DISTILLERY CLOSE-UP. After founder Henry McKenna's death, the ownership of the distillery was passed down to his descendants, including his granddaughter Marcella McKenna. She was one of only a handful of women to own Kentucky distilleries before Prohibition. This close-up view shows the stone one-story building behind the two-story brick distillery. In 1894, the building was marked as being used for bottling and storing used barrels. (Dixie Hibbs.)

TRANSCRIPT FROM WHOLESALE LIQUOR DEALERS' BOOK, Form 52.

...LLED SPIRITS Disposed of by *H. McKenna* , Street, *Fairfield* , *5th* District *Ky*

TO WHOM SENT.	PLACE OF BUSINESS.	NUMBER OF PACKAGES	KIND OF SPIRITS	BY WHOM DISTILLED OR RECTIFIED			BY WHOM AND WHEN INSPECTED 190_			NUMBER OF GALLONS				SERIAL NUMBER AND KIND OF STAMPS					
				Name	Dist.	State	Name	Month	Day	Wine	Proof			Warehouse	Tax-Paid	Rectifiers'	Wholesale Liquor Dealers'	Imported Liquors (Customs.)	Imported Spirits (Int. Rev.)
Jno. Gorin	Bowling Green Ky	1	Whisky	H. McKenna	5th	Ky.	C. E. Hargan	Nov		37.18	38.29			14049	884474	1821554			97%
H. McKenna	For Retail	10	"	"	"	"	J. L. Montgomery	Dec		436.57	436.57			16550-59	406169	1863135			
P. H. Fitzpatrick	Bowling Green Ky.	2	"	"	"	"	C. E. Hargan	Nov			77.36			15243-44					100
J. J. Conlan	New York, N.Y.	1	"	"	"	"	L. C. Roberts			40.63	41.04			18783	674016	1757633			
Purity Supply Co.	Milwaukee, Wisc.	1	"	"	"	"	"			40.44	40.46			18784	17	684			
Campbell & Klotzman	Birmingham Ala.	2	"	"	"	"	J. L. Montgomery	Oct						10730-31					90
Jo Schneider, Jr.	Bowling Green Ky	1	"	"	"	"	"				38.26			13573					97%
McAllister	Lexington, Ky.	1	"	"	"	"	L. C. Roberts	Nov		34.46	34.81			12083		1718991			
			"	"	"	"	"			40.15	40.65			15781	67401	1717651			
John Gorin	Bowling Green	2	"	"	"	"	C. E. Hargan			74.32	75.01			15245-46			370707		97%
H. Delaney & Co.	Chicago Ill	1	"	"	"	"	J. L. Montgomery	Oct		10.00	10.00			10870	7810333	1718517			
Benziger & McGrath	Shelbyville Ky.	3	"	"	"	"	C. E. Hargan	Nov		104.61	104.61			15953-55					
F. McDonough	Newark N.J.	1	"	"	"	"	J. L. Montgomery	Oct		10.00	10.00			10870	7813383	1718517	370708		
Campbell & Klotzman	Birmingham Ala.	2	"	"	"	"	"	Dec		68.64	70.68			10737-38					90%
H. McKenna	For Retail	2	"	"	"	"	"	May		3.09	6.87			7680-81					
Jo Schneider, Jr.	Bowling Green Ky	2	"	"	"	"	"	Dec		74.64	75.39			4493-54					97%
Newton Bros.	Somerset Ky	3	"	"	"	"	L. C. Roberts	Nov		121.91	121.91			15785-87					
		2	"	"	"	"	C. E. Hargan	"		82.99	82.99			15956-57					
F. J. Dillon	Galitzin Pa.	2	"	"	"	"	L. C. Roberts	"		74.62	79.91			15779-80					90%
H. McKenna	For Retail	1	"	"	"	"	"			65.73	68.36			10728-29					
			"	"	"	"	"			32.52	34.07			10733	7813246	1870386			
		1	"	"	"	"	"			33.16	33.81			10735	248	388			
											1647.61								

McKenna Distillery's 1912 Sales. This page for December 1912 shows the wide variety of wholesale liquor dealers who purchased McKenna bourbon. In addition, it shows who inspected the sale as the final step in the government's close supervision to make sure all applicable taxes were paid. Each sale shows a corresponding serial number and warehouse that the bourbon came from. There were numerous sales to dealers in Kentucky, including firms in Bowling Green, Lexington, Shelbyville, and Somerset as well as national sales to wholesalers in New York, Alabama, and Wisconsin. Kentucky bourbon was known across the globe and the product was synonymous with the state, much like Kentucky Fried Chicken was during the latter part of the 20th century. The form was completed and signed by James McKenna, another "member of the firm," according to the form. (Marcella McKenna Distillery Collection, UKSC.)

LABROT & GRAHAM DISTILLERY. This Woodford County distillery dates back to 1812. It was founded by Elijah Pepper, one of the pioneers of the industry. Elijah's son Oscar Pepper hired Dr. James Crow as his master distiller in 1833. Crow is credited with inventing "sour mash" bourbon. This building contained the complete distilling process from the arrival of the grain to the departure of the filled barrels of bourbon. (Brown-Forman Archives.)

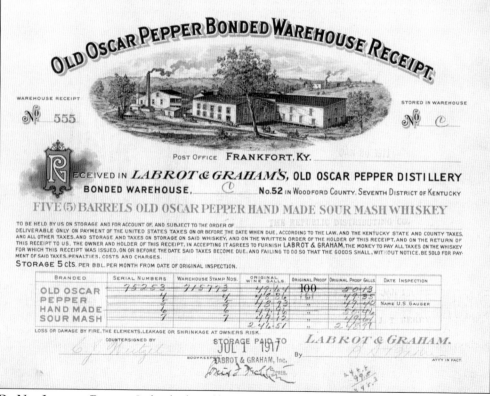

DO NOT LOSE THE RECEIPT. Individuals and businesses could "invest" in barrels of bourbon stored in bonded warehouses at distilleries. They could make a profit when the bourbon was bottled after all the taxes and storage costs were paid. That money helped the distillery owners pay expenses while the thousands of barrels of bourbon aged for years in warehouses. This 1917 receipt is for five barrels of Old Oscar Pepper. (Brown-Forman Archives.)

O·K·H
OLD · KENTUCKY · HOME
WHISKEY

ANDREW HAGAN DISTILLING Co.
LEXINGTON, KY. U.S.A.

HAGAN'S OLD RYE WHISKEY.

Direct from Distillery to Consumer

WHISKEY IN JUGS.

Hagan's Old Rye, Bourbon or Malt; 4 years old; per gallon, $2.00.
Hagan's Old Rye, Bourbon or Malt; 6 years old; per gallon, 2.50.
Hagan's Old Rye, Bourbon or Malt; 7 years old; per gallon, 2.75.
Hagan's Old Rye, Bourbon or Malt; 8 years old; per gallon, 3.00.

WHISKEY IN CASES.

We will send 4 full quarts of Hagan's Rye, Bourbon or Malt, 10 year old for $3.50; 6 full quarts for $5.00 or 12 full quarts for $10.00, packed in plain case (no marks) with corkscrew and etched glass, express charges prepaid.
We do not prepay express charges on whiskey under $3 per gallon.

If You Want Pure Whiskey, Drink Hagan's Rye

SPECIAL PRICE LIST:—We quote the following Brands of whiskies bottled and cased by Stoll & Co., Lexington, Ky.:

Old Elk 4s, 12 bottles per case $15.00.
Old Elk 4s, 6   "   "   7.50.
Old Elk 5s, 12   "   "   14.00.
Old Elk 5s, 6   "   "   7.00.
Bond & Lillard 4s, 12 bottles, per case $15.00.
Bond & Lillard 4s, 6   "   "   7.50.
Bond & Lillard 5s, 12   "   "   14.00.
Bond & Lillard 5s, 6   "   "   7.00.

Old Tarr 5c, 12 bottles, per case $18.00; 6 bottles, per case $6.50.
Ashland 5s, 12 bottle, per case $12.00; 6 bottles, per case $6.00
Old Elk is bottled in bond and also free; the other whiskies are bottled free only. You run no risk whatever in sending us your order. We guarantee every shipment we make to be exactly as represented. If goods are not entirely satisfactory, ship them back and your money will be refunded. We do not ship goods C. O. D. Please make all remittances payable to The Hagan Distilling Company.
References:—The Lexington City National Bank or Stoll & Co., largest distiller in State

Address: THE HAGAN DISTILLING Co.
Lexington, Ky.

ANDREW HAGAN DISTILLING SOLD BY MAIL. Neither the 1894 nor the 1910 Sanborn distillery maps show an Andrew Hagan Distillery in Lexington. It is more likely that the company purchased bourbon and rye from distilleries in Lexington to process into cases of bottles or jugs to sell directly to consumers. This 1901 advertisement is from the *Hazel Green Herald* in Wolfe County. There are several other bourbon whiskies listed besides the featured O.K.H. (or Old Kentucky Home) Whiskey and Hagan's Old Rye Whiskey, including Old Elk and Bond & Lillard. It looks like all the bourbon and rye was obtained from Stoll & Co., which the advertisement claims is "the largest distiller in the State." There was a Stoll Distillery at one time in Lexington, but there was also a very large Stoll Distillery in Louisville. To further muddy the waters, according to an advertisement selling one of the original Andrew Hagan Distilling Co. whiskey jugs, Hagan was a saloonkeeper and liquor dealer in Lexington. (Library of Congress.)

WOMEN AND MEN BOTTLE BOURBON. This early photograph of the bottling crew at the Boone County Distillery shows a mix of women and men. During this time period, women did most of the bottling and labeling at many distilleries, working side-by-side with men. The drawback to this type of work was that it was very seasonal. Most distilleries were only open during the warmer months of the year, when there was no problem with a frozen water supply and farmers had fresh corn and other grains to sell. The Boone County Distillery was located in the town of Petersburg in northern Kentucky. It was a huge facility, processing 2,000 bushels of grains daily during the six months of the year that it was run. It was also different in that it produced sweet mash bourbon and not sour mash whiskey. That meant that no "setback" from the previous batch was added to each new batch. (Boone County Library.)

OLD PRENTICE DISTILLERY VISITORS. These three ladies, accompanied by two young boys, were photographed around 1905 at the Old Prentice Distillery. The large bell they are posing under allegedly came from a Louisville fire station. At one time, it stood in front of the Old Prentice Distillery building erected on the site in 1910, but its current location is unknown. The former Old Prentice Distillery is now the Four Roses Distillery. Four Roses took over the site after Old Prentice went out of business. The Old Prentice brand had been around since 1855. Although "bourbon tourism" had yet to be born and there were no visitor centers or free samples to attract potential customers, it is evident from some of the photos in this book that members of the public visited the distillery sites. (Joseph Seagram & Sons Photographs, UKSC.)

BIRD'S-EYE VIEW OF RIPY BROS. DISTILLING Co. The entire layout of the Ripy Bros. Distillery can be seen in this photograph. It was located in Tyrone, in Anderson County. Although the Ripy Bros. Distillery, which was founded in 1888, is no longer in business, the facility is still in use today by Wild Turkey. Ripy Bros. produced bourbon and rye sour mash bourbon. (James Weddle Photographic Collection, UKSC.)

ONE OF THE RIPY BROTHERS. After graduating from college in 1896, Ernest "E.W." Ripy went to work with his father, T.B. Ripy. They sold the two distilleries they owned in Tyrone to Kentucky Distilleries in 1899. In 1905, E.W. Ripy and his brothers Ezra, Forest, and J.C. built the Ripy Brothers Distillery. The Ripys continued to be involved with J.T.S. Brown after the distillery was sold. (Ripy family collection.)

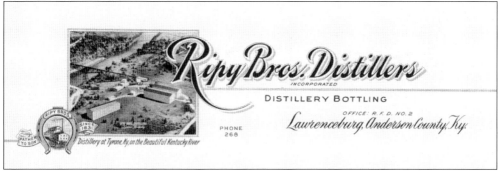

A DISTILLING DYNASTY. In 1869, Thomas B. Ripy and his partner W.H. McBrayer bought a small Anderson County distillery. They made T.B. Ripy Sour Mash there and, along with other distilleries in the area, made Tyrone one of the state's busiest river towns. In 1906, the Ripy-owned distilleries in Tyrone employed about 125 men in various capacities plus 20 women in the bottling department. (Ripy family collection.)

POPULAR DURING THE CIVIL WAR. Jacob Beam's original Old Jake Beam's Sour Mash gave way to Old Tub Whisky in the 1850s. In 1859, David M. Beam, Jacob Beam's grandson, moved the Beam brand from its original home in Washington County to nearby Bardstown. Old Tub was reportedly the most popular bourbon in Kentucky during the Civil War. (Dixie Hibbs.)

Bridge and Boone's Knob — Camp Nelson — 19

LONG COVERED BRIDGE AND STONE DISTILLERY. One of the most attractive small distilleries in Kentucky was the E.J. Curly Distillery, built of limestone on the banks of the Kentucky River at Camp Nelson in Jessamine County. Built in 1880, the distillery's brands included Boone's Knoll, Royal Bourbon, and Blue Grass Bourbon. Adjacent to the distillery in the background is the 240-foot-long, double-barreled wooden covered bridge that was in use from 1838 to 1926. In 1923, during Prohibition, the distillery was converted into a hotel with beautiful views of the river and palisades. After Prohibition, it returned as the Kentucky River Distillery and operated into the 1970s, adding the Old Lazy Days brand to its list. Some of the distillery's warehouses can be seen along the high bank of the river. The warehouses were unusually narrow because of the terrain. (T.P. Curry Photographic Album, UKSC.)

Three

FASCINATING FACES

PAYDAY AT THE DISTILLERY? These distillery workers turned out in the 1890s to have their photograph taken with some of the tools of their trade. The two men flanking the small boy seated at the table are possibly paying the workers since there is a lot of paperwork in front of them. The photograph was probably taken at an Anderson County distillery. (Joseph Seagram & Sons Photographs, UKSC.)

ARCHETYPE OF A "KENTUCKY GENTLEMAN." Col. Robert Perry Pepper (1833–1895) came from a family of distinguished whiskey distillers. He moved from Woodford County to Frankfort and built his own distillery after the Civil War. According to his obituary in the *Frankfort Roundabout*, in 1874, he gave up distilling "and turned his attention entirely to the breeding and developing of fine trotting horses. He bred and raced some of the fastest animals which ever faced a starter." (Pepper Family Collection, UKSC.)

KENTUCKY BELLES AT DISTILLERY. These ladies were photographed at the Harrison County Keller Distillery near Cynthiana, which was known for its landscaped grounds. Most of the young ladies in the photograph are wearing what looks like school uniforms, so perhaps they were on a school outing. The photograph was taken prior to 1920 since the A. Keller Distillery closed in 1920 because of Prohibition and never reopened. (Peggy Carter.)

PAPPY VAN WINKLE WAS ALWAYS A FINE SALESMAN. He coined the brilliant marketing quote, "We make fine bourbon at a profit if we can, at a loss if we must, but always fine bourbon." Julian Prentice "Pappy" Van Winkle Sr. was born in Danville, Kentucky in 1874. He worked as a traveling salesman for W.L. Weller & Sons after moving to Louisville in 1893. After Prohibition ended, he founded the Stitzel-Weller Distillery in Shively near Louisville in 1935. The company flourished for many years but fell on hard times and was sold in 1972. Pappy Van Winkle continued to serve as president of the distillery until his death at age 94. He was followed as president by his son Julian Van Winkle Jr. (Stitzel-Weller Distilling Company Slides, UKSC.)

MEN AND HORSES AT OLD PRENTICE. These two men depended on their team of horses to move barrels of bourbon and other cargo around the Old Prentice Distillery in Anderson County, outside of Lawrenceburg. This type of transport was universal at the distilleries until the advent of the gasoline engine. There was a mill, called Bond's Mill, at the site dating to 1817. Distilling started there in the 1880s. This photograph was taken after J.T.S. Brown & Sons bought the distillery in 1894, but before it was redesigned and rebuilt in a Spanish Mission style. When Prohibition ended, it was owned for a short time by the Julius Kessler Distilling Company before being purchased by Joseph E. Seagram & Sons in 1942. Seagram eventually changed the name to the Calvert Distilling Company, one of their subsidiary companies, and eventually to Four Roses Distillery. (Joseph Seagram & Sons Photographs, UKSC.)

MASH ROOM GROUP PORTRAIT. These men are pictured in the mash room of the J.W. Dant Distillery that was located at Dant's Station, about 14 miles west of Lebanon in Nelson County, near New Hope. The New Hope area, at its peak, had nine distilleries that supported hundreds of families and four rail stops on the Knoxville branch of the Louisville and Nashville (L&N) railroad. The four stops that serviced some of the distilleries were at Gethsemane, New Hope, Coon Hollow, and Dant Stations. The J.W. Dant Distillery started in 1836 when Joseph W. "J.W." Dant started a modest distilling business on his farm. He grew all the grains, grew his own yeast, and even made his own barrels. When his whiskey began to sell, he built a modern distillery in 1870. This photograph was probably taken in the 1930s as electric lights, including small fluorescent light panels near the ceiling, can be seen. (Dixie Hibbs and Oscar Getz Museum of Whiskey History.)

NEAT AS A PIN. These women on the bottling line in the bottling house at Labrot and Graham's Old Oscar Pepper Distillery in their white shirtwaists and matching bows illustrate the cleanliness of the bottling process. The man in the hat is probably a government official, as all steps of the bourbon-making process were monitored by the government to ensure that all applicable taxes were paid. (Oscar Getz Museum of Whiskey History.)

GEORGETOWN COLLEGE ALUMNUS. In 1867, John M. Atherton (1841–1932) built a distillery near the junction of Rolling Fork and Knob Creek in LaRue County. He was elected as a state legislator and was chairman of the Democratic State Central Committee as well as a founding director of the Kentucky Distillers' Association. Atherton was a very successful businessman and made sizeable contributions to his alma mater, Georgetown College. (Dixie Hibbs.)

HARRISON COUNTY DISTILLERY WORKER. This man was only identified as John Lain, pictured about 1890. The photographer was identified as "Redmon, Cynthiana, KY.," so it is probable that Mr. Lain (or Lail) was employed by one of Harrison County's numerous distilleries. On the 1894 Sanborn map, besides T.J. Megibben's distilleries in Lair and two distilleries located in Cynthiana, other Harrison County distilleries were located in Connersville, Berry, and Poindexter. (Joseph Seagram & Sons Photographs, UKSC.)

BOURBON MASH FED FISH. Thomas Beebe Ripy III is seen here with a large buffalo fish, *Ictiobus cyprinellus*, which he caught in the Kentucky River near an outlet that discharged some of the Tyrone distilleries' used mash in the 1950s. Environmental concerns no longer allow the dumping of what might have been a delightful treat for the river's fish although too much would have been toxic. (Ripy family collection.)

THOMAS BEEBE "T.B." RIPY. T.B. Ripy (1847–1902) was the son of an Irish immigrant, James Ripy, who learned whiskey distilling from his father. James built the first distillery in Tyrone, a river town a few miles east of Lawrenceburg in Anderson County. T.B. built an additional distillery there and, by the late 1890s, was known as the world's largest independent sour mash distiller. (Ripy family collection.)

MOTHER AND WIFE OF DISTILLERS. Sarah Elizabeth "Sally" (Fidler) Ripy married T.B. Ripy, and the couple had five sons, including Thomas Beebe Ripy Jr., Ernest Whitney Ripy, James Catlett Ripy, Forest Ripy, and Ezra Ripy and five daughters. After T.B. died in 1902, Sally lived in the large Ripy home in Lawrenceburg for many years, able to enjoy grandchildren and great-grandchildren, some of whom worked in the distilling industry. (Ripy family collection.)

FRENCH LICK SPRINGS, ORANGE CO., IND.

F. N. HUNTON, PHOTO.

1890

RIPY FAMILY ON VACATION. This family portrait was taken in French Lick Springs, Indiana, a popular vacation resort, in 1890. Like many of the families involved in Kentucky's distilling scene at the time, the Ripys were a large, close clan. Thomas B. "T.B." Ripy invested in the distillery his father, uncle, and others had started, and in 1868, the brand T.B. Ripy was first sold. In 1873, T.B. built the Cliff Springs Distillery. In 1881, he built a third distillery, the Clover Bottom Distillery. He then owned three distilleries in Anderson County. In 1902, the Ripy distilleries were bought by the Kentucky Distillers and Warehouse Co. (the Whiskey Trust). The next generation of Ripys entered the business as this was happening. The Ripy family had ties to several distilleries in Anderson County, but Prohibition shut them all down in 1920. Some members of the Ripy family are still involved with distilling today. (Ripy family collection.)

OLD FITZGERALD WORKER. This photograph shows an unidentified worker near the old wooden mash tubs of Old Fitzgerald Bourbon. The brand dates back to 1870, when it was produced by John E. Fitzgerald in Frankfort. It was marketed to railroad and steamship lines and private clubs. The brand Old Fitzgerald was purchased by Pappy Van Winkle after Prohibition, and it was produced at the Stitzel-Weller Distillery using a new formula that Van Winkle introduced that added a "Whisper of Wheat" to the original formula, according to advertisements. The brand continued to be produced at Stitzel-Weller until 1992, when Stitzel-Weller closed and production was then transferred to the Bernheim Distillery. Heaven Hill purchased the Bernheim Distillery in 1999 along with the Old Fitzgerald brand and continues to produce it today. (Stitzel-Weller Slides Collection, UKSC.)

DID IT PRODUCE TINY BOTTLES? This was identified as a "working" model of the Glenmore Distillery in Owensboro, but no information was available on whether bourbon could actually be made. The man proudly showing off the model is unidentified. The original Glenmore Distillery was built between 1868 and 1871. Through the years, it became one of the largest independent distilleries in America. (Charles Manion Collection, Kentucky Room, Daviess County Public Library.)

MEDLEY DISTILLERY BIG-WIGS AND FRIEND. The two men in this 1950s photograph are identified as Tom Barker (left) and Ben Medley. Their canine friend is Captain. The two men are looking at the automatic control on the still and doubler at the Medley Distillery in Owensboro. There were several generations of the Medley family who worked in the distilling business in Daviess County over several decades. (Lawrence Hager Collection, UKSC.)

IT WAS NOT ALL WORK. Stitzel-Weller master distiller William H. McGill and his dog Chief were photographed in 1948 relaxing after a hard day's work. Above McGill's head is a sign that says, "No chemicals allowed. Nature and the old-time 'know how' of a master distiller get the job done here." Many called him "Will," but around the Stitzel-Weller distillery he was called "Boss." McGill was the master distiller in charge of making some of the finest bourbon ever and believed in making whiskey "the old-fashioned way." Before coming to Stitzel-Weller in 1934, he worked with Tom Moore and Early Times in Nelson County. Will McGill and Pappy Van Winkle were of the mutual opinion that distilling whiskey was more art than science and that the "old fashioned school of sour mash bourbon, the rule-of-thumb method" was best. He died in 1952 at the age of 87, having reached the title of "oldest living executive distiller in the country." (Photograph by Lin Caufield, courtesy of Sally Van Winkle Campbell, from *But Always Fine Bourbon: Pappy Van Winkle and the Story of Old Fitzgerald.*)

Four

BEFORE AND DURING
PROHIBITION

SALOONS WERE COMMON IN PRE-PROHIBITION PARIS. There were 16 saloons in 1908 Paris, including Connelly's Saloon on Main Street. Pictured here is owner James Connelly (at right). Another Paris saloon owner in 1908 was French Thompson, an African American man who also owned a saloon on Main Street. Saloons disappeared across Kentucky with Prohibition in 1920, but some reappeared upon its repeal in 1933. (Hopewell Museum.)

LEXINGTON'S NICK RYAN'S SALOON. Another victim of Prohibition was Nick Ryan's Saloon in Lexington, although the name has been used by restaurants until recently. The saloon's signs promised that Bond & Lillard Whisky was available inside. Bond & Lillard was a trusted name in the pre-Prohibition whiskey industry. It was first distilled by John Bond in what was then called Cedar Run, in Anderson County, in 1820. A veteran of the American Revolutionary War, Bond soon moved his distilling operation closer to Lawrenceburg. By 1849, W.F. Bond, John's son, partnered with his brother-in-law Christopher Lillard. Lexington also produced several well-known bourbon brands, including those distilled at the large local distilleries including the James E. Pepper Co. Distillery, the Ashland Distillery, and the Commonwealth Distillery. (Lexington, Kentucky Photograph Albums, UKSC.)

WOMEN'S MARCH FOR PROHIBITION. The first part of the 20th century was rife with political activism in Kentucky and the rest of the nation. Women, especially, often led the way in pressing for suffrage for women, temperance, and even prohibition of alcohol, as this women's march in Cynthiana exhibits. One sign was as true then as it is now: "You Can't Fool the People All the Time!" (Anne Griswold.)

THE KENTUCKY WHITE RIBBON. A popular newspaper published by the Kentucky Woman's Christian Temperance Union, headquartered in Owensboro for more than a decade, fought for temperance/prohibition and women's suffrage. The motto beneath the masthead reads, "No Sex, No Shirks, No Simpleton in Citizenship." It is fairly clear what they mean about not wanting shirking or simpletons, but the same cannot be said for "No Sex." (UKSC.)

STATE UNIVERSITY PROHIBITION CLUB. The idea for prohibition was well accepted by many Kentuckians before its passage in 1920, as this 1914 photograph of sober collegians in Lexington exhibits. Their school was known as the Agricultural & Mechanical College of Kentucky from 1878 to 1908, when its name was changed to State University. After 1916, the school in Lexington was called the University of Kentucky. (Glass Plate Negative Collection, UKSC.)

PROHIBITION FACTS. This advertisement appeared in the November 29, 1918, issue of the *Bourbon News* in Paris after the Kentucky General Assembly had already ratified the 18th Amendment by a joint ballot of 94-17, on January 14, 1918. Ironically, a state known as the home of bourbon became the first "wet" state to ratify the Prohibition amendment to the Constitution. Thousands of jobs were lost as a result, and tax revenues declined. (Library of Congress.)

BARROOM MURDERS BLAMED ON LIQUOR. A bloody fight in Paris that killed two and seriously wounded another was blamed on liquor sold at a saloon and those who wanted the tax money saloons generated for the city. This advertisement was found in the September 11, 1914, edition of the *Bourbon News*: "Last week from a saloon on Main Street was a trail of blood on the pavement for two blocks. Maybe the injured man ran into the door, maybe he fell, but you know what might have happened. To every saloon in Paris can be traced streams of blood, fresh and still warm. Now the saloon keeper is endeavoring to wash it away, before you, Mr. VOTER, shall see it." Similar to other advertisements across the state, it was politically motivated. "You Mr. Voter shall say on September 28th if lives are to pay the toll of the saloons." (Library of Congress.)

THE TRUTH

About the Saloon!

+++++++++++++

More Human Lives Added To The Toll of The Liquor Men of Paris.

We judge the thing, if it is good or bad by its results. That is a principle of business. Let us judge the saloon, the agent of the liquor traffic in Paris by its results.

On last Saturday evening three men, inflamed with whisky, which was bought in a Paris saloon, engaged in a quarrel, and as the result two men are now forever beyond the pale of the saloon, cold dead corpses, another near deaths door. Who these men were does not matter, but they were some one's son, some one's brother, whether black or white. Their lives were worth $16,000 per year. Is not the life of your father or brother worth more than the tax on liquor men give Paris? In the past week count for yourself the men who are lying in their graves as the result of these saloons. The actions of men inflamed by whisky, sold by the saloon keeper, licensed by the town, approved by the voter, you the voter, You Mr. VOTER shall say on Septmber 28th if lives are to pay the toll of the saloons.

Last week from a saloon on Main street was a trail of blood on the pavement for two blocks. Maybe the injured man ran into the door, maybe he fell, but you know what might have happened. To every saloon in Paris can be traced streams of of blood, fresh and still warm. Now the saloon keeper is endeavoring to wash it away, before you, Mr. VOTER, shall see it.

Are you proud of this record of the past few weeks?
Is this saloon and bloodshed "TRUE TEMPERANCE?"

(Advertisement)

79

CARRIE NATION BIRTHPLACE, GARRARD COUNTY, NEAR LANCASTER, KY.

Carrie Nation's Kentucky Birthplace. Carolyn "Carrie" (or "Carry") Amelia Moore was born in this house in Garrard County, near Lancaster, on November 25, 1846. Her father farmed in Kentucky and was also a livestock dealer. The family moved a lot during her youth (1846–1865), living across Kentucky, Texas, and Missouri. Ill health curtailed Carrie's formal education. (Postcard Collection, UKSC.)

CARRY A. NATION AND HOME

Nation's Home in Medicine Lodge, Kansas. Carrie Moore married Dr. Charles Gloyd in 1867, whom she left because of his alcoholism in 1868, before the birth of their daughter later that year. After his death, she remarried in 1877 to David Nation, a lawyer and minister. He, too, was a temperance activist. Her full name was Caroline Amelia Moore Nation, but she was almost always referred to as Carrie, sometimes also spelled "Carry." (Postcard Collection, UKSC.)

CARRIE NATION

"HATCHET GRANNY." Carrie Nation is remembered today as the face of the national temperance movement, especially for her signature attacks on alcohol-serving establishments using a hatchet before the advent of national Prohibition (1920–1933). She was arrested many times for destroying property, but it was in a famous 1904 incident in Elizabethtown, Kentucky, that she was the abused party. The saloonkeeper named Neighbors attacked Nation with a chair twice after she gave a temperance lecture at his front door. While many considered Nation unhinged and fanatical, the publicity she garnered for the movement she championed was invaluable. She died in 1911, but while she never got to see the fruits of her labors, Nation's loud voice contributed to the passage of the 18th Amendment. (Library of Congress.)

NELSON COUNTY 1926 MOONSHINE STILL. This illegal distilling operation was busted by Internal Revenue agents in Nelson County. The still was set up next to a creek that provided the necessary water for the mash liquid and cooling water. Records of still seizures during Prohibition indicate the volume of moonshining in Kentucky: an annual average of 675 stills were seized, 2,799 arrests were made, 21,681 gallons of distilled spirits were confiscated, 424,564 gallons of mash were confiscated, and 217 vehicles were seized. The IRS was originally assigned as the enforcement agency for the Prohibition Amendment and the commissioner of the IRS set up the Prohibition Bureau. The bureau's agents had broad powers of enforcement which included the authority to punish wrong-doers with fines and prison terms. In addition, they could confiscate "rum-running" cars, boats, and other vehicles. (Dixie Hibbs.)

FOR MEDICINAL USE? During the lean years of national Prohibition (1920–1933), J.T.S. Brown and Sons was allowed to sell some of its already warehoused Old Prentice through a special license held by Frankfort Distilleries for "medicinal use." This label gives the location of the distillery as McBrayer, Kentucky, the closest post office to the facility. Patients were limited to a certain amount of whiskey every 10 days. (Joseph Seagram & Sons Photographs, UKSC.)

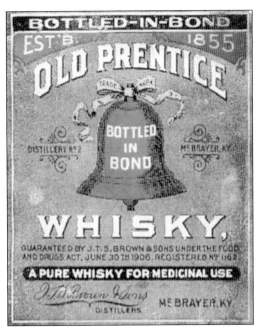

WHISKEY POURED DOWN THE SEWER. Old Lewis Hunter whiskey, distilled in Cynthiana in Harrison County, remained in the news even in the midst of Prohibition. This photograph appeared in the *Indianapolis Times* in 1924. The Indiana story said that "several bottles of Old Lewis Hunter Rye are slated to be poured down the sewer" by the local sheriff. Times were tough for liquor drinkers and sellers. (Library of Congress.)

EDITORIAL CARTOONS ABOUNDED. The editorial page cartoons in newspapers were a popular form of commentary in America for many years, and Prohibition provided lots of fodder. This cartoon that ran in September 1919 was drawn by John C. Comacher and was titled "The Sacred Cider Grove." The caption under the cartoon read, "Are these good eatin apples?" "No, mister; not this year they ain't. This year them apples is good drinkin' apples." That referred to the ability of farmers with apple trees to produce hard cider to keep from having to worry about a source of alcohol after national Prohibition began in 1920. While the cartoon might have been seen as amusing, it illustrated one of several problems that did not amuse the national government at all: how to enforce national Prohibition when some of the still-drinking public had access to impossible-to-monitor homemade liquor, and the rest were making law-breakers rich. (Library of Congress.)

MULE-RIDING UNDER THE INFLUENCE? There is not a lot of information about this photograph, only that it was taken in the 1930s. It looks like a lot of men in cars and trucks have "pulled over" the man riding the mule who is holding a bottle of liquor. Enforcement of the Prohibition Amendment was first assigned to the IRS and later to the FBI. They could confiscate cars, boats, and other vehicles used in rum-running, but no one can confirm the confiscation of a mule. Since making whiskey legally was illegal, for the most part, during Prohibition, whiskey drinkers had to look elsewhere for their tipple. An unintended consequence of national Prohibition was the rise of organized crime, which stepped in to provide a profitable commodity. Shoot-outs and car chases were other unwanted side-effects of the law. (UKSC.)

SAM CLAY WHISKEY BY DOCTOR'S ORDERS. This whiskey was expressly produced for family and medicinal use by Julius Kessler & Company. This may have been the origin of the phrase that a drink is "good for what ails you." Kessler bought out several Bourbon County distilleries, including the Paris Distillery, which produced Sam Clay Whiskey. During Prohibition, a doctor's prescription for whiskey was a must-have for those who wanted to continue to drink the amber fluid. Although modern medicine tends to dismiss the patient's actual need for whiskey, 100 years ago, doctors did believe that whiskey helped with pain management, could heal chronic diseases, and fight infections. Countless Westerns showed the good guy being offered a slug of liquor to dull the pain before the "sawbones" removed a bullet. Even up through the end of the 20th century, parents believed in rubbing whiskey on a baby's gums to help soothe teething pains. (Authors' collection.)

PROHIBITION'S "NOBLE EXPERIMENT." America's great social and legal blunder began on January 16, 1920. Although much of Kentucky's warehoused bourbon would be sold for "medicinal use," only a small amount of legal bourbon distilling was allowed in the state. Hundreds of distilleries in many counties were closed forever, and thousands of workers were out of work just as the world's Great Depression was beginning. The effects on the farming industry were equally dire – suddenly the reliable market for millions of bushels of grain disappeared. The early days of Prohibition created a few photo opportunities like this one, showing cases of Old Ripy and Old Taylor being put to the axe. Prohibition ended on December 5, 1933, and the Ripys and other distilling families returned to the business. However, many small distilleries did not reopen, and others did not succeed during the coming age of "big business." (Ripy family collection.)

REFORMING AMERICA WITH A SHOTGUN

A Study of Prohibition Killings

Prepared by the

ASSOCIATION AGAINST THE PROHIBITION AMENDMENT

NATIONAL PRESS BUILDING
WASHINGTON, D. C.

•

Research Department
JOHN C. GEBHART, *Director*

Second Edition, October, 1930

"REFORMING AMERICA WITH A SHOTGUN." Founded in 1918, the Association Against the Prohibition Amendment (AAPA) was among the leading political pressure groups that worked to secure the repeal of the 18th Amendment. Their continued pressure on Congress and pamphlets like this one hurried repeal in 1933. As organized crime syndicates grew throughout the Prohibition era, territorial disputes often transformed America's cities into violent battlegrounds. Homicides, burglaries, and assaults consequently increased significantly between 1920 and 1933. In the face of this crime wave, law enforcement struggled to keep up. Prohibition ultimately failed because most of the adult population wanted to continue drinking, policing was riddled with contradictions, biases, and corruption, and the lack of a specific ban on consumption hopelessly muddied the legal waters. In their propaganda, the "Drys" had promised that a national Prohibition amendment would create a more lawful, industrious, and harmonious society. Measured against these standards, Prohibition failed disastrously. (Library of Congress.)

Five

BOURBON BOOM
AFTER PROHIBITION

GETTING READY FOR LEGAL DISTILLING. Although many distilleries never reopened again after Prohibition ended in 1933 and were "lost" to Prohibition, others did reopen, including the James Pepper Distillery in Lexington. The demand for bourbon and rye whiskey was heavy, and the inventories in warehouses had been drawn down during the period between 1920 and 1933. The Pepper Distillery was purchased by the Schenley Products Corporation in 1934. (Lafayette Studio Photographs, UKSC.)

UP IN FLAMES! This April 1934 photograph shows the James Pepper Distillery in flames not long after construction had begun at the facility. Hopefully, the Schenley Products Corporation had good insurance, since most of the large complex was damaged or destroyed in the massive blaze. The corporation was rebuilt, and soon, the Schenley Products Corporation was one of the largest distillers in the country. (Lafayette Studio Photographs, UKSC.)

CROWD VISITED THE SMOKING RUINS. Entertainment was harder to come by in the 1930s, before television and smartphones, so the site of a huge fire was a draw for residents. This is a photograph of a group who turned out to see what was left of the James Pepper Distillery in Lexington. Smoke can still be seen coming off some of the piles of rubble. (Lafayette Studio Photographs, UKSC.)

FIRE DAMAGE SCENE. The iconic tall smokestack with "Jas. E. Pepper" on it at far left in this photograph looks mostly undamaged, but numerous other (mostly warehouse) buildings look like they were completely destroyed by the April 1934 fire. If there was a silver lining to the disaster, it was that the normal distillery workforce had most likely not started work yet since the construction work was ongoing. It would be some months until the facility could be rebuilt so that the distillery could begin producing sour mash bourbon again after a 14-year hiatus. The bourbon made in 1934 would have to age for several years before it could be bottled and sold, so distillery owners needed deep pockets to weather the years when money went out for construction, payroll, and raw materials and nothing came in. For a country still mired in the Great Depression, coming up with the large investment needed was even more difficult—one of the reasons so many distilleries never reopened when Prohibition ended. (Lafayette Studio Photographs, UKSC.)

SCRATCH-AND-DENT SALE? Just seven months after the disastrous fire at the James Pepper Distillery in Lexington, another catastrophe occurred when a warehouse full of bourbon barrels collapsed in November 1934. Most of the barrels that can be seen look undamaged. Many bourbon warehouses had racks that were marked as "patented" on the Sanborn maps and were of various heights from three to eleven barrels high. (Lafayette Studio Photographs, UKSC.)

LEXINGTON-MADE BOURBON HEADED FOR CALIFORNIA. This sign, most likely on a railroad car, proves that Col. James Pepper was a good salesman. He traveled extensively in the United States, promoting his bourbon. Pepper claimed that his bourbon was "the first and the best." His claim as "first" dates back to his grandfather Elijah Pepper, who was most likely one of the first to produce corn-based whiskey in the state. (Lafayette Studio Photographs, UKSC.)

JAMES PEPPER DISTILLERY REOPENS AFTER PROHIBITION. Unlike many of the bourbon distilleries across the state, the Jas. E. Pepper & Co. Distillery reopened after the industry-blighting nightmare of Prohibition was over. The sign on the side of the warehouse says that it was the "FIRST Bourbon Made in Kentucky," which linked the bourbon produced there to the bourbon made by Elijah Pepper in his distillery near Glenn's Creek in Woodford County in the late 1700s. James Pepper was Elijah Pepper's grandson and claimed to use some of his family's historical bourbon recipes, but using that claim for the James Pepper Distillery that opened in 1889 seems a bit of a stretch. The distillery closed in 1967 and sat abandoned until 2017, when bourbon began to be produced again at the now-renovated distillery. Saving the facility after 50 years of disuse was possible since some of the original buildings remained. (Lafayette Studio Photographs, UKSC.)

MIDWAY DISTILLERY. This photograph was identified as being of the "Mr. J.H. Byrd (Distillery) Midway" when it was taken in 1933. Looking into the history of the Midway Distillery, it is probable that Byrd owned the construction company tasked with rebuilding on the distillery's site when Prohibition ended. Midway Distillery took over the site in 1916 and stayed in business until the distillery was destroyed by fire in 1924. (Lafayette Studio Photographs, UKSC.)

NEW BOURBON WAREHOUSE. This 1933 photograph shows a bourbon warehouse under construction by the J.H. Byrd Construction Company in Midway. The brick walls have been constructed and this view shows the interior of the warehouse being built. The floor has yet to go in as the new lumber is resting on the grass. The wealth of distilleries rested and aged in thousands of warehouses like this around Kentucky. (Lafayette Studio Photographs, UKSC.)

SNAZZY CAR AT MIDWAY DISTILLERY. What looks like a new 1933 automobile is in this photograph taken that year at the Woodford County Distillery. The newly built garage also houses a couple of cars and what looks like a buggy near the back door. It is likely that J.H. Byrd contracted with the Lafayette Studio in Lexington to photograph the buildings his company constructed so he could show them to potential clients. (Lafayette Studio Photographs, UKSC.)

EXTERIOR OF THE PARK & TILFORD DISTILLERY, 1943. In 1941, Park & Tilford Distillers Incorporated, a New York corporation that already owned distilleries in New York, Pennsylvania, and Louisville, acquired the Woodford County Distillery located in Midway. One of their marketing items was a bronze-colored coin showing a jockey on a Thoroughbred on the front and a horseshoe on the back with the slogan "A Winner At The Right Price." (Lafayette Studio Photographs, UKSC.)

COMPANY BANQUET. This photograph was taken in January 1944, of the Park & Tilford Distillers' management group and their wives enjoying a holiday season banquet celebrating a successful 1943. Park & Tilford was a New York Corporation that purchased two distilleries in Kentucky: one in Louisville and one in Midway. The company wanted to be able to market its straight whiskey and blended whiskey as having a Kentucky connection. (Lafayette Studio Photographs, UKSC.)

BOURBON AT REST IN MIDWAY. These bourbon warehouses had metal one-piece shutters that could be opened and closed depending on the weather. In the warehouse in the middle of this 1946 photograph, most of the shutters can be seen to be opened. Park & Tilford owned the distillery in 1946, and controlling the conditions in the warehouses was an important decision that affected the taste of the final product. (Lafayette Studio Photographs, UKSC.)

WATER LAGOON AT PARK & TILFORD. The Park & Tilford Distillery was located on Lee's Branch, a tributary of Elkhorn Creek, in Midway. However, at least up through the 1910 Sanborn map, the water that served the distillery's needs was not from the creek but instead, a spring and wells. When this photograph was taken in January 1946, the water for the distillery's needs was collected in this large water lagoon seen in the foreground. Perhaps the water was filtered or aerated or perhaps just held in the lagoon so it could be kept in motion enough to keep it from freezing. Earlier distilleries could only operate a few months out of the year because their water sources were prone to freezing in the winter weather and they also could not obtain fresh grains from farmers. From 1941 to 1954, the Park & Tilford Distillery thrived, but times grew rough for the bourbon industry and the corporation sold the distillery to the Schenley Corporation in 1958. They closed the distillery for good in 1959. (Lafayette Studio Photographs, UKSC.)

Stitzel~Weller Distillery
INCORPORATED

NUMBER

B. 3547

0

In accordance with the Federal Alcohol Administration Act (August 29, 1935) the distilled spirits covered by this warehouse receipt shall be packaged before delivery in bottles labeled and marked in accordance with law or be delivered in bulk only to persons to whom it is lawful to sell or otherwise dispose of distilled spirits in bulk.

REGISTERED DISTILLERY NO. 16   SHIVELY, KY.

Shively, Kentucky July 16, 1959

Received in our Internal Revenue Bonded Warehouses No. 16, located in Shively, Kentucky, in the Seventh District of Kentucky, for account of and subject to the order of

John Doe, 1400 West Main Street, Louisville 1 Kentucky

Deliverable only upon (a) the surrender of this warehouse receipt, properly endorsed, and (b) payment to the undersigned of United States Government taxes, and all other taxes of every character and description assessed against or that may constitute a lien upon said whiskey, and all license and other taxes that now or hereafter may be imposed upon the undersigned because of the storing, warehousing, withdrawing, bottling, or other handling of the aforesaid whiskey, and (c) the payment to the undersigned of all unpaid storage and handling charges and such other charges that may hereafter accrue in connection with the withdrawal and delivery of the whiskey. Storage charges hereunder shall be at the rate of eighteen cents (18c) per barrel per calendar month or fraction thereof to October 1, 1958 and twenty-one cents (21c) per barrel per calendar month or fraction thereof thereafter.

Storage, state, county and local ad valorem taxes on the within described whiskey accrue from   **June 16, 1959**

THE FOLLOWING DESCRIBED: **FIFTY (50)   BARRELS KENTUCKY SOUR MASH WHISKEY**

BRANDED	DATE TAX PAID	SERIAL NUMBERS	PROOF	ORIGINAL TAX GALLONS	WHEN MADE	TIME FOR REGAUGE EXPIRES	FED. EXCISE TAX DUE
SOUR MASH BOURBON		760869-918	103	2,504.5	June 16, 1959		June 15, 1979

This warehouse receipt is issued upon the following terms and conditions, which are to be binding upon the present owner and holder hereof and upon each and every assignee or subsequent holder hereof:
1. The United States Government taxes upon aforesaid whiskey shall be payable to the undersigned whenever said whiskey shall be withdrawn from bond unless said whiskey has theretofore been removed in bond from the warehouse of the undersigned, and all other taxes and charges hereinabove referred to shall be payable to the undersigned upon the removal of said whiskey from its warehouse.
2. On the expiration of four years from the date of production as aforesaid whiskey, other than the United States Government taxes and all accrued storage charges shall be and become payable to the undersigned; thereafter on the first day of January and the first day of July, in each year, all accrued taxes, other than United States Government taxes and all storage charges on said whiskey shall be paid and if any of such charges are not paid, as hereinabove provided, within thirty (30) days after the same shall become due, the undersigned shall have the right upon giving notice as required by law, to sell said whiskey at public sale, and apply the proceeds of sale toward the payment of said storage charges and any other charges that may have accrued against said whiskey and toward the payment of all taxes constituting a lien upon said United States Government taxes and all other taxes and charges hereinabove referred to, shall be and become at once payable to the undersigned, and should said charges remain unpaid for thirty (30) days, then the undersigned, after giving notice as required by law, may proceed to the sale of said whiskey at public sale, and may become the purchaser for its own account at such sale.
3. It is hereby expressly agreed that the undersigned shall be and is absolved from any and all liability or risk of every kind in case of loss or damage to the said whiskey resulting from the elements, fire, riot, accidents, theft or any cause beyond its control.
4. This receipt is issued on condition that the delivery of said whiskey shall be made only as authorized by law and by such regulations, whether made pursuant to federal or state authority, as may be issued with respect thereto. The undersigned warrants that the whiskey covered by this receipt is packaged in new, heavily charred, white oak barrels, and has not been treated by any quick aging process.
Uninsured—owner's risk.

COUNTERSIGNED

STITZEL-WELLER DISTILLERY
INCORPORATED

By _____   KENTUCKY PRODUCTION TAX PAID   By *Julian P. Van Winkle*
PRESIDENT · VICE PRESIDENT · SECRETARY · TREASURER

BOTTLED IN BOND RECEIPT. When Stitzel-Weller sent 50 barrels of their good sour mash whiskey to their warehouse in 1959, they completed this certificate agreeing to keep the barrels secured, under government supervision, until they bottled it or for 20 years; whatever came first. And until then, they did not have to pay taxes on it. The Bottled-in-Bond Act of 1897 laid out requirements that had to be met in order for a whiskey to be labeled as "bottled-in-bond." These stringent legal requirements include that the liquor must be produced in one distilling season by one distiller at one distillery and aged for at least four years in a government-supervised bonded warehouse. Col. E.H. Taylor Jr. was instrumental in getting the bill passed in 1897. (Joseph Seagram & Sons Photographs, UKSC.)

A LOOK BACK AT STITZEL-WELLER. This 1959 photograph of men rolling barrels out of one of the warehouses at Stitzel-Weller was taken during the period between when it was founded in 1935 and when it was sold in 1972. The company flourished during that era, at its height employing more than 200 people and producing 800,000 cases of bourbon a year. (Photograph by Lin Caufield, courtesy of Sally Van Winkle Campbell, from *But Always Fine Bourbon: Pappy Van Winkle and the Story of Old Fitzgerald*.)

EVEN THE BARRELS WERE SPECIAL. This 1959 photograph of the inside of Stitzel-Weller's cooperage shows longtime cooper George Durkalski (right) as he made barrels the old-fashioned way using tools like those that might have been used on the *Mayflower*. The Stitzel-Weller barrels were thicker than many others and used eight metal hoops instead of the more common six. (Photograph by Lin Caufield, courtesy of Sally Van Winkle Campbell, from *But Always Fine Bourbon: Pappy Van Winkle and the Story of Old Fitzgerald*.)

OLD LEWIS HUNTER DISTILLERY. This November 1934 photograph of the Old Lewis Hunter Distillery is taken from a different angle than most. It was taken from the opposite bank of the South Fork of the Licking River showing the trees reflected in the water and the distillery complex in the background. The Old Lewis Hunter Distillery was located near Lair's Station in Harrison County. (Lafayette Studio Photographs, UKSC.)

BOURBON WAREHOUSE UNDER CONSTRUCTION. Business was booming for Kentucky distilleries as they raced to fill the pent-up demand for legally produced bourbon and whiskeys that were safe to drink. This warehouse construction project in 1935 at the Old Lewis Hunter Distillery near Cynthiana, was only one of many such projects happening all over the state. Perhaps "Happy Days Are Here Again" could be the timely slogan. (Lafayette Studio Photographs, UKSC.)

BUSY WHITE FRAME DISTILLERY OFFICE. Now that Prohibition was finally over, all facets of Kentucky distilleries had to restart after a 13-year-long hiatus. Although, of course, making and storing the bourbon and rye whiskey was of utmost importance, so was keeping track of the taxes paid and deferred as well as all the materials that had to be kept on hand so that production could run smoothly, which all happened in this office. (Lafayette Studio Photographs, UKSC.)

MASH TANKS BUBBLING AWAY. Fermentation is taking place in the large mash tanks at the Old Lewis Hunter Distillery in this May 1935 photograph. Overseen by the two men (center), the tank on the left is full and working, and the tank on the right is either being filled or being cleaned before a new batch arrived. Lots of open windows provided sunlight and fresh air. (Lafayette Studio Photographs, UKSC.)

OLD LEWIS HUNTER'S SECOND-FLOOR STILL. A workman can be seen in this photograph taken in May 1935. The grain hopper, seen at the center of the image, was used to fill the vats with grain for the mash. To make a fermentable base, distillers mixed grains—corn (at least 51 percent), rye or wheat, and barley malt—with water and yeast. This is called the "mash." (Lafayette Studio Photographs, UKSC.)

PACKING UP THE DRIED SPENT MASH. The bourbon-making process produces a lot of used mash. Most distilleries fed the spent mash, which contained nourishing grains, to livestock. Others, like the Old Lewis Hunter Distillery, dried at least a portion of their used mash to be sold as livestock feed. A uniformed distillery worker can be seen here in 1935 in the drying room at the Harrison County distillery. (Lafayette Studio Photographs, UKSC.)

LOTS OF BOURBON BARRELS. This photograph was taken at the Old Lewis Hunter Distillery in 1935. It shows a bourbon warehouse with a single layer of barrels. That is unusual, as most bourbon warehouses had wooden racks, or "ricks," built in to hold several levels of barrels in order to maximize the number of barrels that could be held in each warehouse. (Lafayette Studio Photographs, UKSC.)

A SINGLE BARREL. This barrel of Old Lewis Hunter Distillery Co. Incorporated's bourbon whiskey was filled on October 6, 1936, after the failed experiment of Prohibition had died a quiet death. The barrel head shows that the distillery was located in Lair in the Seventh District. It was inspected by J.T. Rawlings, storekeeper and gauger, according to the information stenciled on the barrel head. (Lafayette Studio Photographs, UKSC.)

DISTILLERY COMPLEX IN LAIR. The Old Lewis Hunter Distillery plant can be seen in the foreground and the distillery's warehouses are visible in the background in April 1938. Newspaper advertisements that year touted Old Lewis Hunter bourbon as "Handmade Kentucky Bourbon for 77 Years." That linked the present concern with all the previous distillers who had made bourbon on that site. (Lafayette Studio Photographs, UKSC.)

RUN, BARRELS, RUN. Several men can be seen moving barrels along a barrel run that was used to move the heavy, filled barrels from the distillery to the warehouses. The six-story warehouse has a large "F" above the door, which indicates that the distillery had at least six bourbon warehouses when this photograph was taken in 1938 at the Old Lewis Hunter Distillery in Harrison County. (Lafayette Studio Photographs, UKSC.)

1941 Virginia Newspaper Advertisement. The *Roanoke Rapids Herald* carried this advertisement in March 1941 for the Old Lewis Hunter brand of "Kentucky Straight Bourbon Whiskey." The label features a large bald eagle logo. The price for the five-year-old bourbon is quite inexpensive at $1.35 per pint and $2.60 per quart. The distillery had made more rye than bourbon before Prohibition, but it looks like they switched to straight bourbon whiskey when the distillery got back up and running after Prohibition. The smaller copy in the middle of the ad reads, "Distilled in Harrison County, the heart of the Kentucky Blue Grass district, with limestone water, by the identical process and formula since 1861." Distilleries tended to use links to historical distillers in their marketing efforts and perhaps stretched the truth a bit, but, in most cases, bourbon recipes did not change much through the years and customers could count on the same taste from their favorite bourbon year after year. (Library of Congress.)

"GREEN RIVER—WHISKEY WITHOUT A HEADACHE." J.W. McCulloch started making his Green River Whiskey in 1885, and it was good enough to be awarded a grand prize at the Liège Exposition in Belgium in 1905. An after-hours fire in 1918 at the distillery destroyed all the whiskey and most of the buildings. This put the once very successful distiller out of business until after Prohibition. In 1936, the property and brand were sold to Kentucky Sour Mash Distilling Company. After rebuilding the facility, the company also had to declare bankruptcy. It was in 1939 that members of the Medley family from Owensboro stepped in and purchased the facility, forming the Medley Distilling Company. They continued for nearly 70 years, making the smooth drink until 1970. Green River Distilling Company has recently been revived by J.W. McCulloch's great-grandson, still promising "Whiskey Without A Headache." (Above, Lafayette Studio Photographs, UKSC; below, Courtesy Dixie Hibbs.)

J.T.S. BROWN'S SON CO. IN TYRONE. In 1948, when this photograph was taken, this sign would have told visitors that they had already arrived if they were looking for the distiller, bonded warehouse, bottler, or rectifier. A rectifier is a distillery that uses bourbon from other distilleries to blend and bottle. Numerous well-known distillers started as rectifiers using bourbons from one or more distilleries to achieve a desired taste profile. (Lafayette Studio Photographs, UKSC.)

OLD BRAND IN NEW LOCATION. The J.T.S. Brown label had been around 100 years when the owners moved it to the old Ripy plant in 1955. In this 1960s photograph, J.T.S. Brown employees (from left to right) Billy Noel, Orville Robinson, Charles Buntain, Chink Moore, Ike Case, Mike Adams, and Jim McGinnis are seen in the filling and weighing room. (Ripy family collection.)

LABELING BARRELS. Before barrels were stored away in warehouses, they had to be properly dated, numbered, and labeled, as J.T.S. Brown Distillery workers Mike Adams (left) and Jim McGinnes are doing. The information was unique to each barrel, as it included a serial number and was stenciled onto the filled barrels. Some early distilleries had a stencil furnace to heat the stencil that was burned into the barrel head. (Ripy family collection.)

MEMORABLE BARREL. E.W. Ripy Jr. (left) and Orville Robinson are seen here in 1961 with the 400,000th barrel of J.T.S. Brown made in Anderson County. The J.T.S. Brown label has been around since 1870, when John Thompson Street Brown introduced it in Louisville. It was made by the Ripys from the 1950s to the late 1970s. It is now made by Heaven Hill in Bardstown. (Ripy family collection.)

We believe the reason **Old J.T. S. Brown** is one of Kentucky's **favorite** whiskies is because it offers people of this great state the **best** value. The name Old J.T.S. Brown has been associated with the fine traditions and culture of Kentucky for **over 100 years.** Each drop of this old style sour mash is made and bottled in **our own** Kentucky **distillery.** We believe it is our obligation to the very many who have accepted Old J.T. S. Brown as the **greatest** value in **taste** quality and **price** available... to maintain the traditional policies of distilling and marketing which have established our product's **leadership.**

J. T. S. BROWN'S SON CO. INC. • LAWRENCEBURG, KENTUCKY

ADVERTISEMENT WORTH MORE THAN 1,000 WORDS. It is said that "a picture is worth a thousand words." This clever magazine ad that was run in the 1950s (which some people say was the heyday of print advertising) is a picture and 103 words. This advertisement was run in a Kentucky publication and plugs that connection, saying that Old J.T. Brown Kentucky Straight Bourbon Whiskey offers the people of Kentucky "the best value" and that the name Old J.T. Brown "has been associated with the fine traditions and culture of Kentucky for over 100 years." There were numerous distilleries and brands that incorporated the word "old" into their name. The goal was to try and indicate the brand was historic and time-tested. Hardly anyone wanted to be seen as "new," even if they were. The whiskey's name, J.T.S. Brown, even made its way into two books by Walter Tevis: *The Hustler* and *The Color of Money.* (Ripy Family Papers, UKSC.)

AN INSIDE LOOK. A tornado that roared through Lawrenceburg and the J.T.S. Brown Distillery in November 1965 provided this cutaway look inside a bourbon barrel warehouse. The barrels were stored in racks (or ricks) usually three high that are designed for good air circulation. Many of the warehouses that dot Central Kentucky are six to nine stories high and contain as many as 20,000 barrels. Each distiller has different requirements for their warehouses; some want them on top of hills, and some in valleys. Some rickhouses are heated, and some are not temperature controlled at all. In the latter category, some distillers may rotate their barrels as the bourbon ages while some prefer to blend the whiskey from the warmer top floors with the contexts of a barrel from the cooler floors below to achieve a consistent product. (Ripy family collection.)

GLENN'S CREEK HISTORIC DISTILLING SITE. This postcard from the 1930s provides an aerial view of Glenn's Creek south of Versailles, where three different distilleries had facilities. Old Taylor, Old Crow, Labrot & Graham, and Elijah Pepper, along with other bourbons, had historic ties to the area. The Old Taylor Distillery, with its long line of barrel warehouses at the top of the photograph, is the one pictured here. (Postcard Collection, UKSC.)

WOMEN AT WORK PACKING AT NATIONAL DISTILLERIES. Women were often employed bottling or packaging bourbon whiskey, as this 1944 photograph illustrates. National Distilleries was created during Prohibition from American Medicinal Spirits, which was formed from the old Whiskey Trust. National owned brands like Old Crow, Old Taylor, Sunnybrook, Old Grand-Dad, Mount Vernon Rye, and Old Overholt. (Lafayette Studio Photographs, UKSC.)

COLUMBIA AMERICAN DISTILLERS. This little-known distillery was located in Owensboro in Daviess County and produced Old Monroe five-year-old bourbon sometime after Prohibition. The slogan for Old Monroe was "As Mellow As The Moonlight." These photographs were taken in the 1950s after it was acquired by Glenmore Distilleries. Today, an Old Monroe bourbon and rye is produced in Missouri. At one time, Daviess County was home to several large distilleries. Owensboro and the area around Owensboro was where most of the large distilleries were clustered because of the access to the river and railroads that was available there. Farther out in the county, one of the smallest distilleries was located at Newman, Kentucky, according to the 1910 Sanborn map. The J.D. Wheatley Distillery there had a mashing capacity of only 13 bushels per day. (Both, Lawrence Hager Collection, UKSC.)

SNOWY GLENMORE DISTILLERY. This 1950s view of the sprawling Glenmore Distillery in Owensboro was obviously taken during the winter, as the trees at the far right are covered in snow. The original Glenmore Distillery was built, owned, and operated by R. Monarch. It was built between 1868 and 1870. After Prohibition, the distillery grew larger and by the 1950s, it was processing more than 6,000 bushels of grain daily. (Lawrence Hager Collection, UKSC.)

MULTI-MILLION-DOLLAR 1938 FIRE. This photograph shows three telephone company linemen working on a line in front of the Glenmore Distillery during a fire there in November 1938. The multi-million-dollar fire completely destroyed a six-line bottling house. After the fire, an old building containing three bottling lines was used. It was expanded until in 1951, Glenmore was using nine bottling lines. (Historic Photograph Collection, Kentucky Room, DCPL.)

NARROW-GAUGE RAILROAD AT GLENMORE. Since the Glenmore Distillery facility in Owensboro was so large, reaching a capacity of 6,000 bushels per day at its height, this narrow-gauge railroad must have made transporting barrels around the distillery easier. Glenmore was sold to James Thompson in 1901, and upon his death in 1924 the ownership passed to his sons Col. Frank Thompson and James P. Thompson. The distillery's main brand was Kentucky Tavern, and in 1944 it acquired Yellowstone Bourbon. Not only was the distillery itself a large employer in Owensboro, but it also had a large cooperage that, in 1957, employed 150 people. At one time, Glenmore was recognized as one of the largest independent distilleries in the country. The company passed through numerous hands after the Thompson family sold out in 1991. It is owned by Sazerac today, and they utilize the Glenmore plant as a bottling facility. (Kentucky Room, Daviess County Public Library.)

MEDLEY DISTILLING FACILITY IN OWENSBORO. The Medley family of Daviess County has been involved in making whiskey for more than 200 years. Possibly known as Daviess County Distilling after Prohibition when this photograph was taken, Medley Distilling was located on a one-mile-long section that once contained distilleries that included John Hanning, Green River, Rock Springs, M.P. Mattingly, and Daviess County Distilling. (Charles Manion Collection, Kentucky Room, DCPL.)

MEDLEY'S LAST POT STILL. Pictured in front of the distillery office in 1960 is the last copper pot still, also known as a "batch still," used by the Medley Distillery in Owensboro before the company changed over to the more efficient column or continuous stills. That transition was made by most of the distilleries in the state because of the larger volume of bourbon being made. (Charles Manion Collection, Kentucky Room, DCPL.)

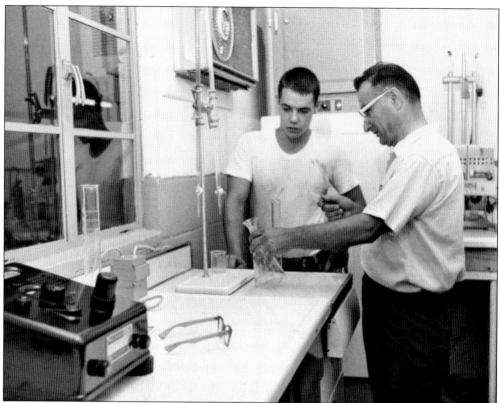

LAB AT MEDLEY DISTILLERY. Pictured here at the Medley Distillery laboratory are John Mark Medley (right) and ? Cherolis. Distilling whiskey is recognized as an art and a science. Labs like this one generated the accurate scientific data needed to answer questions about purity, quality, safety, and regulatory compliance. The Daviess County Distilling Company was begun in 1873 and was purchased by George Medley in 1901. (Lawrence Hager Collection, UKSC.)

MEDLEY COMPANY 1956 LETTERHEAD. The Medley family claims an eight-generation history of making bourbon in the state, and they have been in Owensboro and Daviess County since 1878. The Medleys intermarried with another Kentucky distilling family, the Wathens, who distilled the famous Old Grand-Dad brand in their Nelson County distillery. It melded into Medley Distilling Company in 1940 and finally closed in 1991. (Lawrence Hager Collection, UKSC.)

Six

RIVERS TO RAILS

BOURBON GOING UP OR DOWN RIVER. Riverboats on the Ohio River were still an important way to transport goods around 1900 when this photo was taken in Carrollton of barrels of Old Darling Bourbon being loaded. Since many Kentucky distilleries were located on rivers, riverboats made sense as a means of transport. Eventually, the railroad and modern trucks sank the riverboat industry. (Oscar Getz Museum of Whiskey History.)

H.S. CHAMBERLAIN. The H.S. *Chamberlain* (1911–1929) was one of many paddle-wheel steamboats that traveled the navigable rivers of Kentucky carrying consumer goods, agricultural produce, and lots of barrels of bourbon whiskey produced at distilleries situated close to the rivers. This boat was built at the Howard Ship Yards in Jeffersonville, Indiana, at the cost of $18,500 and traveled the waters of the Kentucky, Tennessee, and Ohio Rivers. (Louis Nollau Collection, UKSC.)

RIVERBOAT CAPTAIN. Capt. W.H. "Harve" Phillips was the master of the H.S. *Chamberlain* for many years and probably visited the docks of numerous distilleries over his tenure, picking up and delivering the supplies to produce Kentucky bourbon and the final product itself. Captain Phillips looks like he would be right at home in one of Mark Twain's riverboat stories. (Louis Nollau Collection, UKSC.)

RIVERS WERE EARLY HIGHWAYS. At the beginning of the 20th century, there were more than 130 steamboat landings on the Ohio River between Frankfort and Carrollton and an additional 37 landings upriver from Frankfort to Shakers Landing. The boats carried passengers, livestock, and all the various products that the mostly rural families that were served could use or produce. They also provided an essential, commercial shipping service for bourbon distilleries. (Louis Nollau Collection, UKSC.)

BIGGER RIVERS PROVIDED ACCESS TO WORLD. While the Kentucky River and other navigable "interior" waterways provided contact within the state, bigger rivers like the Ohio and the Mississippi opened up the rest of the nation and the world as a possible market for bourbon. Louisville, Newport-Covington, and Maysville were major "big river" shipping ports for Kentucky bourbon. (Central Kentucky Photograph Albums, UKSC.)

Paddle-Wheeler Passing under Young's High Bridge. This fully loaded paddle-wheeler can be seen passing under the Louisville Southern Railway bridge over the Kentucky River built in 1889 and called Young's High Bridge. The bridge connected Anderson and Woodford Counties. There were no supports in the river to interfere with the passage of the riverboats that plied up and down the river carrying passengers and cargo during that period. The span stands 258 feet above the water. The buildings on the right bank are part of the small town of Tyrone. It was originally a river town that grew much larger with the addition of several bourbon distilleries in the neighborhood. A couple of those distilleries were owned by members of the Ripy family, who named the town after the county in Ireland where the family emigrated from. (Ripy family collection.)

A Whole Box Car Full of Bourbon. This photograph was taken at the James E. Pepper Distillery in Lexington and shows several men loading cases of bourbon whiskey into the railroad car. The big shipment was on its way across the country to San Francisco, California. Bourbon was exported from Kentucky to every corner of America and internationally. The shipment of bourbon was a steady source of income for the railroads, and many of the larger distilleries had railroad sidings that brought the train cars right to the doors of the warehouses where they delivered raw materials and picked up freshly packed boxes of full bourbon bottles. When the main form of transportation became trucks, railroads in Kentucky began to die. Trucks were much more flexible and could go to lots of places that railroad tracks could not. (Lafayette Studios Photographs, UKSC.)

GRAIN ARRIVAL BY TRAIN CAR. There had to be a steady stream of corn and other grains pouring into the distilleries in order for them to keep producing bourbon. This train car is unloading grain at the James Pepper distillery in Lexington. Millions of bushels of grains, including mostly corn but also rye and wheat, were sold by Kentucky farmers to nearby distilleries. Malted barley, another key ingredient for bourbon and rye whiskies, was sometimes purchased from large, out-of-state companies. A few of the larger distilleries had their own malt house to process the barley into malt. The ups and downs of the whiskey market also affected the thousands of farmers across the state who sold their crops to distilleries. When Prohibition became law in 1920, it produced a ripple effect throughout Kentucky, which was home to more distilleries than any other state. Distillery workers, farmers, truck drivers, railroad employees, and other workers all lost jobs or regular sources of income. (Lafayette Studio Photographs, UKSC.)

SHORT-LINE RAILWAY SERVED DISTILLERIES. The Frankfort & Cincinnati Railroad never reached the Ohio city in its name, but before Prohibition, the railway provided a critical link for distilleries between Frankfort and Paris. The 40-mile long short-line railroad terminated in those two towns but had connections at both ends with the Louisville & Nashville (L&N) Railroad. The line, then known as the Kentucky Midland Railway, was completed in 1890. The name was changed to the Frankfort & Cincinnati Railroad in 1899. It was nicknamed the "Whiskey Route" because it served several distilleries, especially in the Frankfort area. Shown in the photograph is the F&C engine No. 100 in Paris. After business declined steadily, the F&C went out of business in the 1960s. (Ken Hixson, from *Forty Miles, Forty Bridges: The Story of the Frankfort & Cincinnati Railroad*.)

MAINTAINED THE TRACKS OVER WHICH BOURBON ROLLED. Pictured here sometime before 1937 is a section crew of the F&C Railroad in Bourbon County that maintained the tracks and bridges between Paris and Georgetown. It was headed by foreman A.M. "Albert" McClain (right). He took over as foreman from his father, John A. McClain, and three of his sons also worked for the F&C Railroad maintaining tracks. Most of those tracks have been taken up and sold as scrap metal. The last few decades of the 1800s and the first two decades of the 1900s were the pinnacle for Kentucky railroads. Moving the grains and empty barrels to the distilleries and picking up cases of bottled goods or full barrels for transport to connecting railways that serviced the entire country, was big business. As with many of the ancillary industries, national Prohibition did much, along with the more flexible trucking industry, to kill almost all the railroads in Kentucky. (Ken Hixson and Virgil McClain.)

Seven

SHUTTERED, SILENT, OR REPURPOSED

SPLENDID LANDMARK STRIPPED. In 1989, the stone Kentucky River Distillery in Jessamine County was dismantled for its building material and to make room for development. The 70-acre property once held bourbon warehouses, cattle sheds, and grain storage facilities, all tucked in beneath the cliffs along the river. It was known by many names since the 1870s when it was built, including E.J. Curly's, Camp Nelson, and Boone's Knoll. (Postcard Collection, UKSC.)

LEXINGTON SALOON REPURPOSED AS CITY OFFICE. Before Prohibition, Lexington, Kentucky's second-largest city, had more than 100 saloons, or one bar for every 300 citizens. After the enactment of the 18th Amendment, this old saloon was turned into the city planner's office. After 1920, it was hard to get a drink in Lexington, which was once one of the state's largest producers of whiskey and beer, unless one knew the secret knock. (UKSC.)

BEAUTIFUL STONE DISTILLERY BECOMES A HOTEL. The Kentucky River Distillery was repurposed after Prohibition began into a hotel. Many of the rooms offered beautiful views of the river below. It also overlooked the Camp Nelson covered bridge (the Hickman Bridge) over the Kentucky River. Constructed in 1838, the bridge was condemned in 1926 after a truck crashed through the roadbed and replaced with the iron bridge seen at far right. (Oscar Getz Museum of Whiskey History.)

GORGEOUS SETTING FOR DISTILLERY AND HOTEL. When this photograph was taken sometime after Prohibition began, this site along US Route 25, had been utilized as a distillery for one of the state's premier sour mash bourbons; it was repurposed as a hotel and then returned to being a distillery. It was dismantled in 1989. Prohibition destroyed more than this beautiful building, as thousands of jobs, hard-earned capital, and general respect for the law were also lost. (UKSC.)

BOURBON WAREHOUSE REPURPOSED. Bourbon warehouses owned by Stoll, Clay & Co. Distillery (opened in 1880) located in Sandersville, just northeast of downtown Lexington on Georgetown Road, were closed in 1919 just before Prohibition. The sturdy, brick warehouses were repurposed by the venerable Hillenmeyer Nurseries in Fayette County. Lexington has a long history of bourbon-making dating back to the Ashland Distillery, which was the first registered distillery in Central Kentucky. (Clay Lancaster Collection, UKSC.)

DISCOVER THOUSANDS OF LOCAL HISTORY BOOKS
FEATURING MILLIONS OF VINTAGE IMAGES

Arcadia Publishing, the leading local history publisher in the United States, is committed to making history accessible and meaningful through publishing books that celebrate and preserve the heritage of America's people and places.

Find more books like this at
www.arcadiapublishing.com

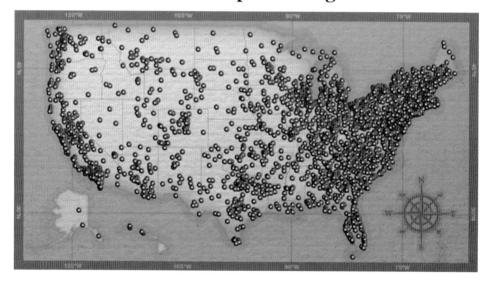

Search for your hometown history, your old stomping grounds, and even your favorite sports team.

Consistent with our mission to preserve history on a local level, this book was printed in South Carolina on American-made paper and manufactured entirely in the United States. Products carrying the accredited Forest Stewardship Council (FSC) label are printed on 100 percent FSC-certified paper.

MADE IN THE

USA